C000097829

the Idler

ISSUE 37 | SPRING 2006

First published in Great Britain in 2006

10 9 8 7 6 5 4 3 2 1

The Idler, Issue 37
© copyright Idle Limited, 2006

First published by Ebury Press, Random House, 20 Vauxhall Bridge Road, London SW1V 2SA

Random House Australia (Pty) Limited
20 Alfred Street, Milsons Point, Sydney, New South Wales 2061, Australia
Random House New Zealand Limited
18 Poland Road, Glenfield, Auckland 10, New Zealand
Random House South Africa (Pty) Limited
Isle of Houghton, Corner Boundary Road & Carse O'Gowrie,
Houghton, 2198, South Africa
The Random House Group Limited Reg. No. 954009
www.randomhouse.co.uk
A CIP catalogue record for this book is available from the British Library.

The views expressed by the contributors do not necessarily reflect those of the editors.

Cover illustration by Andrew Council
Text design and typesetting by Gavin Pretor-Pinney

ISBN 0091906229
ISBN 9780091906221 (from January 2007)

Papers used by Ebury Press are natural, recyclable products made from wood grown in sustainable forests.

Printed and bound in Germany by Appl, Wemding

Editor: Tom Hodgkinson   Creative Director: Gavin Pretor-Pinney
Deputy Editor: Dan Kieran   Managing Editor: Clare Pollard
Editor at Large: Matthew De Abaitua
Literary Editor: Tony White   Sports Editor: John Moore
Music Editor: Will Hodgkinson
Contributing Editors: Greg Rowland, Ian Vince
Advertising: Jamie Dwelly at Cabbell 020 8971 8450
For editorial enquiries call 020 7691 0320

THE SCHOOL BOY

I love to rise in a summer morn
when the birds sing on every tree;
The distant huntsman winds his horn,
And the skylark sings with me;
O what sweet company!

But to go to school in a summer morn,
O it drives all joy away!
Under a cruel eye outworn,
The little ones spend the day
In sighing and dismay.

Ah then at times I drooping sit,
And spend many an anxious hour;
Nor in my book can I take delight,
Nor sit in learnings bower,
Worn through with the dreary shower.

How can the bird that is born for joy
Sit in a cage and sing?
How can a child when fears annoy
But droop his tender wing,
And forget his youthfull spring?

O father and mother, if buds are nipped,
And blossoms blown away;
And if the tender plants are stripped
Of their joy in the sprining day,
By sorrow and care's dismay,

How shall the summer arise in joy,
Or the summer fruits appear?
Or how shall we gather what griefs destroy,
Or bless the mellowing year,
When the blasts of winter appear?

William Blake, Songs of Experience

THE BIG SUN
THE BUBBLE
THE ATOMIC AFTERMATH

THREE GENERATIONS
OF LIFE IN POST-WAR JAPAN

KATIE KITAMURA

JAPANESE FOR TRAVELLERS

OUT ON 25 MAY 2006

www.hamishhamilton.co.uk

IN CONVERSATION WITH MICHAEL PALIN 64

CONTENTS THE IDLER
Issue 37, Spring 2006

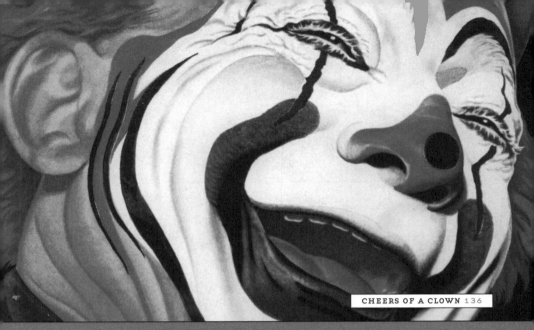

CHEERS OF A CLOWN 136

CONTENTS THE IDLER
Issue 37, Spring 2006

THE PRACTICAL IDLER

EDITOR'S LETTER

T he problem with education is not that there is not enough of it but that there is far too much of it. As is the case with work, more does not mean better, and in fact a rise in quantity generally produces a decline in quality. Government presents itself as having the nation's best interests at heart when it says that more education is needed and that they will pour more money into education. More, more, more. But who does all this extra education serve? It is doubtful whether education really does educate, in the sense of stimulating the mind and the body and instilling a passion for being alive, or whether it simply gives the user a certain level of literacy and numeracy in order to work and consume (let's say, you need to be taught how to fill in a job application form and type your credit card numbers into a website). Education would also in most cases seem to encourage a lifelong distate for study, poetry, science and the arts. I can't wait to quit school, we think, and get on with the serious business of earning money in order to play Playstation whenever I want, and not to have to read William Blake.

So it goes that school successfully diverts us away from the great revolutionary, rebellious spirits of the last two thousand years, by fooling us into thinking they are boring. I imagine that if The Beatles were taught at school, we would avoid them like the plague when we left.

The long days at school also bore the teachers and bore the kids. Bertrand Russell was of the opinion that two hours with children at a time is enough for any adult. If teachers only worked four or five hours a day, or two or three days a week, they would be more likely to enjoy teaching. They would be less tired and less stressed. Similarly for pupils, if attendance was made compulsory only from nine till one each day, then the pupils would be less likely to resent school and

to run away from it.

Too much schooling also discourages an independent spirit: if you are accustomed to having your day scheduled for you by someone else, then you are less likely to be able to live free and live independently, as you will always at some level be searching for an outside authority to order your time for you. Less education would lead therefore to more autonomy.

Less education would also reduce the enormous shelling out by the treasury. We should raise teachers' wages and spend less on those wasteful, over-priced bits of digital chalk called computers.

The answer therefore would be to introduce half days all round. So says the *Idler*! Down with skool!

Tom Hodgkinson
Tom@idler.co.uk

IDLER CONTRIBUTORS

Who are the Idlers?

IAIN AITCH is the author of *A Fete Worse Than Death*

MATTHEW APPLETON is the author of *A Free-Range Childhood: Self-Regulation at Summerhill School* (Gale Centre)

STEPHEN ARMSTRONG is a freelance journalist, poet and freedom fighter

GRAHAM BURNETT is an anarchic gardener and runs spiralseed.co.uk

BILLY CHILDISH is a painter, musician and poet

MATTHEW DE ABAITUA is always available

BRIAN DEAN runs the excellent website anxietyculture.com

NICKY SQUIDBUNNY DEELEY once came home and her house was filled with bees, she now lives at www.squidbunny.net

BILL DRUMMOND is a serial father

HANNAH DYSON draws anthropomorphic creatures and other beings

GILES GODWIN is an optimist and a photographer. www.gilesgodwin.com

PAUL HAMILTON regrets nothing, not the divorce, the bankruptcy, the homelessness or the prison record. He would do it all again, except sit through *Love Actually*. No, he does not have a website

CLARE HATCHER is an illustrator from Wiltshire

ANTHONY HAYTHORNTHWAITE is an illustrator for hire, to contact him email anthony@aqhthestudio.co.uk

TOM HODGKINSON is the editor of this magazine. His new book *How To Be Free* is out in August

SANDRA HOWGATE lives in East London and loves to draw. And instead of owning a dog, she takes lines for long walks.

TONY HUSBAND is an award winning cartoonist who works for the *Times*, the *Express*, the *Sun*, *Private Eye* and many many more. For more information visit tonyhusband.co.uk

ADAM JACOT DE BOINOD is the author of the best-selling *The Meaning of Tingo* (Penguin)

SARAH JANES is managing bands in Brighton

FANNY JOHNSTONE writes about sex and cars in the *Daily Telegraph*

DAN KIERAN edited *Crap Towns*, *Crap Jobs* and *Crap Holidays*. He has two books out this autumn, *The My Way Code* with Boxtree and *I Fought The Law* with Transworld

CHLOE KING is an illustrator. She can be reached at chloeking@f2s.com

KIRK LAKE is a writer who spends far too long in second-hand bookshops. musician.

NICHOLAS LEZARD is a critic and does the Slack Dad column in the *Guardian*

JOHN LEGGE is a photographer based in Nottingham, recently specialising in allotment sheds. He digs Nikon cameras and holidays

PETE LOVEDAY created the legendary Russell comics. Find out more at ccnewz.com

MARK MANNING is sometimes Zodiac Mindwarp

KATIE MASKELL has just quit her job, hooray!

JOHN MIERS can be found at houseofslab.com

JOHN NICHOLSON is a historian and sometime model

MARCUS OAKLEY still likes Garibaldi biscuits

KEVIN PARR is a writer and angler. He recently became a white van man.

BP PERRY has ulcerative collitis and butchers piglets for fun. His website is bpperry.com... please don't visit it

FRANKIE POULLAIN was formerly the bass-player of The Darkness

RACHEL POULTON is a mother and photographer

GAVIN PRETOR-PINNEY is the founder of The Cloud Apprecition Society. His book, *The Cloudspotter's Guide*, is published by Sceptre.

GREG ROWLAND is a legitimate businessman

GWYN VAUGHN ROBERTS lives in Wales and can only produce work when his mental state is a fine balance of energy and misery

IAN VINCE is a left-handed, Mac-compatible, asthmatic comedy writer, clearly looking for some kind of niche market. He runs socialscrutiny.org

WALSHWORKS illustrations can be found at www.eastwing.co.uk and www.walshworks. org.uk

CHRIS WATSON has a new t-shirt label at www.tonuppress.com and his work can be seen at www.chris-watson.co.uk

GED WELLS is Insane. See him at www.insane.org.uk

ROB WESTWOOD has recently realised that he is part of the problem

TONY WHITE is the Idler's Literary Editor. He's just co-edited (with Matt

Thorne and Borivoj Radakovic) a new fiction anthology called *Croation Nights*, which is published by Serpent's Tail

MARK WHITE worked on *Adbusters* and now lives in Australia

CHRIS YATES is a legendary fisherman, photographer and master of idleness. His book *How To Fish*, Hamish Hamilton, is out in November

CLOCKWISE FROM TOP LEFT: FRANKIE POULLAIN (ON FAR RIGHT) WITH HIS BROTHERS; SIR JOHN MOORE; IAN VINCE; SARAH JANES; GAVIN PRETOR-PINNEY; WILL & TOM HODGKINSON; JOHN NICHOLSON

NOTES FROM THE COUCH

JEFF HARRISON

THE IDLER'S DIARY

CHURCH OF SAINT MONDAY

It's always nice to inspire the foundation of a new religion, so we were delighted to discover the Church of Saint Monday. Named in honour of the great British tradition of skiving on Mondays, the church takes our book *The Idler's Companion* as its scripture, and the following as its commandments, or "suggestions" as they are described: "I. Thou shall find or invent a job that lets you work when you want. (If that's not an option, see #'s 2-10.) II. Thou shall work to live, not live to work. III. Thou shall partake of the coffee klatch. IV. Thou shall not be forced into middle management. V. Thou shall take sick days. VI. Thou shall use all thy vacation days. VII. Thou shall goof off with thy co-workers. VIII. Thou shall be wary of thy boss. IX. Thou shall honor May Day. X. Thou shall find creative ways to lengthen thy lunch break." All ideas well worth supporting, we think, and you can take a look at www.redroachpress.com/CSM.index.htm

IN HER DEBT

We salute Anya Kamenetz, the 25 year-old *Village Voice* journalist and author of a new book called *Generation Debt: Why Now Is A Terrible Time To Be Young* (Riverhead). Based on a series of pieces she wrote for the *Voice*, the book provides a depressing snapshot of a generation enslaved and disabled by massive credit card bills and college tuition fees. The answer, as should be clear to any idler, is to not bother going to university and to not buy all the consumer crap. Then we won't have to work so hard.

ANYA KAMENETZ

BE A CLOUDSPOTTER

You've checked out the website, you've bought the t-shirt, you've watched him on *Richard and Judy*, now is the time to buy Gavin Pretor-Pinney's book *The Cloudspotter's Guide* (£12.99, Sceptre). www.cloudappreciationsociety.org.

ALL THAT A CLOUD GAZER DESIRES

WORK ISN'T WORKING

Changes to incapacity benefit provoked the biggest backbench rebellion of Tony Blair's first term in office. Years later and with a much smaller majority, he is once again scratching a familiar itch: the belief that millions of people claiming incapacity benefit could be working, but just don't want to.

Last year, in a final salvo as welfare secretary, David Blunkett said that people on incapacity benefit should stop watching daytime TV and start looking for work. The government's rhetoric is now softer but its proposals still fail to address the deeper problems of modern work culture.

The traditional image of the UK's 2.7 million incapacity benefit claimants is of mid-dle-aged men whose jobs in mining, ship-building and manufacturing are long gone. £76.45 a week allows them to spend time tending the allotment, fishing, running the social club, maybe earning a few pounds on the side. Cajoling these men into competing with their sons and daughters for jobs in supermarkets and call centres would require an enormous effort and huge government expense. And to what end?

A newer—and growing—group of claimants is much younger, and includes a larger proportion of women. These are people suffering from stress or depression, often exacerbated by work-related burn-out. They are just the most visible tip

JEFF HARRISON

of an iceberg: everyone who suffers the long-hours, low pay, deskilling and job insecurity that are the dark side of the so-called flexible labour market.

Whatever new tests are introduced for incapacity benefit and whatever assistance and incentives are offered get people back into work, the government is ignoring the fundamental fact that for many millions of people, work is degrading, alienating and miserable.

Jack Thurston

SCOT FREE

Idler contributor Jock Scot has never bothered with working for a living, or competing with others, and now aged 53 he has released his second LP, which we would highly recommend. *Caledonian Blues* features musical contributions from Gareth Sager, formerly of the Pop Group. It is on the Invada label and is distributed by Cargo. Amble out and buy it.

MOORCOCK AND MOORE

To the Blackwells-sponsored promotional event for Michael Moorcock's long-awaited new novel, *Vengeance Of Rome*. His bibliography is expansive, containing a variety of universes, and *Vengeance Of Rome* is the completion of his Colonel Pyat sequence.

As editor of *New Worlds*, inventor of Jerry Cornelius and the author of *Dancers At The End Of Time*, Moorcock

opened up a new direction in science fiction back in the 1960s.

Heavily influenced by Moorcock's work, Alan Moore went on to transform the superhero comic with *V For Vendetta* and *Watchmen* before declaring himself a magician. Both men have contributed to the *Idler*; both are anarchists with first hand experience of small press; it is hard to think of two authors who share such a similar outlook who also happen to sit jacket-to-jacket on the library shelves. Their work recently intersected with Michael Moorcock writing issues of Alan Moore's "Tom Strong" character, a loving return to the Golden Age of pulp.

The chance to eavesdrop on a conversation between two icons of the British counterculture packs out the Jerwood Vanbrugh Theatre in RADA. To begin with, Moore asks about Moorcock's upbringing in the rubble of the Blitz. His father had run off with a lady from his office, leaving the young Moorcock with five books, including Edgar Rice Burroughs *The Master Mind Of Mars* (1928) that had a pronounced influence on his innocent imagination, rewiring his mind just as his own writing would rewire the young Moore. Equally potent was the war itself. The family home was between three air bases. "I actually remember dogfights," says Moorcock. "I watched the searchlights and Ak-Ak guns. My mother held me up so I could see it all."

"It strikes me," observes Moore, "that imagination as much as anything was flattened by the Blitz."

Moorcock agrees. "The 1950s was the greyest period of all time. Romanticism was a man in a raincoat," he adds, thinking perhaps of the figure of Humphrey Bogart in *The Big Sleep* (1946) as the closest the mainstream came to escapism.

"Modernist fiction didn't do it for you if you'd lived through World War Two," he explains. "The likes of Jim [JG] Ballard, coming out of a Japanese POW camp, had no connection with the world of Virginia Woolf."

Both Moore and Moorcock are completely uninhibited when it comes to the scale of their projects. For *Vengeance Of Rome*, Moorcock wanted to examine "how we as a human race had allowed the Holocaust to take place". Alan Moore's novel *Voice Of The Fire* is twelve chapters set in Northamp-

MICHAEL MOORCOCK

ton from 4000 BC to 1995 AD, each written in a voice that takes pains to be historically accurate. To practitioners of literary fiction, these wild and epic swipes invite artistic hubris. They are offensive to a decorous sensibility in which the author most only address that which he or she has some experience of.

Moorcock tells an anecdote about how he held forth about the National Health Service in a Texan bar. A man-fridge of a cowboy came over to him. "He was massive. He could take both me and Alan in a fight." Alan Moore instinctively went to disagree, silently bridling at the suggestion that there was something beyond his powers. It reminded me of what I love about the work of both these writers; the glorious ambition, the bold politics, the big ideas, the license to roam across science, philosophy, history and genre, the refusal to be constrained or dictated to. Then the two men took up their walking sticks and left the stage, each looking like a character from the other's stories.   **Matthew De Abaitua**

READERS' LETTERS

Idleness can be found in work. This issue, three readers give their accounts of slack jobs

DEAR IDLERS,

Having found a seemingly little-known a way to more idle life, I'd like to share it. A year ago I chose to move from the five-a-week day shifts at the office where I work, to twelve-hour 7pm-to-7am night shifts, working two-on three-off then three-on four-off. Most people's reaction to this was to ask me if I'd gone mad, and I wasn't sure if I might be making a mistake, but it turned out to be the best decision I ever made, and as this kind of shift-pattern is becoming more common, especially in offices, I'm writing to suggest that idlers everywhere to consider doing the same thing.

Before I start though, I should add some caveats. Firstly, getting used to sleeping in the day, after working through the night, can take a while; I recommend using foam noise suppressing ear-plugs (available at most chemists) to help with this. There are also, apparently, physical health risks involved with working at night-although I haven't noticed any ailments, and by accepting a night-shift work pattern, you're playing a part in the move toward a 24-hour work cycle, where rest and sleep are devalued.

However, I'd be loath to give up the benefits my shift-pattern offers. First of all, I never have to get up in the morning. Never! My shifts start at seven pm, so I can go out drinking the night before I'm due to work and I have plenty of time to sleep it off before I have to go in, and even if I haven't been out the night before I still have lots of time between waking up and starting work to relax and drink tea, instead of rushing around at a horrible hour of the morning.

Secondly, since my shift plan changed recently to two-on, three-off, I now have three whole days off after every two shifts. I realise how fortunate I am to be paid a full-time wage for this, and that most companies' night-shift employees have to work three or four shifts in a row before getting an equal amount of days off, but even that, in my view, is vastly preferable to normal working hours, ie the five days work for a measly two days rest that was described in Idler 35 as "criminal". Now I have lovely big expanses of free time to luxuriate in, and as my rest days often fall on week days, when the streets are quiet.

Finally, work itself is so much more bearable. I don't have to wear a shirt and tie any more-the old excuse for dress-fascism that "customers might be visiting" doesn't hold sway at night-and there are rarely any supervisors around. The night shift attracts non-conformists; people who, like me, can't be arsed to get up early, or just want to get all their unavoidable work-time out of the way in one go, with the minimum of stupid corporate nonsense involved. I no longer dread going to work, and while I can understand anyone balking at the thought of twelve hour shifts, in this relaxed atmosphere they pass much more quickly than you'd think. Even on the way home, things are better than they were in day-shift purgatory-I drift back to my flat while people around me are hurrying to work, then fall asleep soothed by the sound of the rest of the world rushing about.

I can't recommend it highly enough.

Jamie

Write to us at: **The Idler**, Studio 20, 24-28A
Hatton Wall, London EC1N 8JH or tom@idler.co.uk

DEAR IDLERS,

I truly believe I have the perfect job for idlers.

I work for a small engineering company who supplies labour to the rail industry. All I can say is, No wonder the railways are in such a shite state!

For example, last week I was rostered to be on site at 4pm until 4 am. When we arrived the boss did not know what we were supposed to be doing, nor did we. We sat in our van drinking coffee until 11.20 that evening. By that time you have lost the will to work, it is cold, you are in a nice warm van swapping stories and watching silly video clips on phones, watching dvds etc. In fact we were idling without even thinking about it. We had to get out of the van for 20 minutes then the boss let us go. What a waste of our time, his time, Notwork Rail's time and the cost. Well, a van full of blokes idling for ten hours was worth a small fortune.

I am happy to idle. I will idle away on a shift and take several hours fetching a shovel with no intention of actually using it. I get paid to idle.

Long live the rail industry and I strongly recommend, not a career in it but a way of earning enough to survive on. I used to work five days, 9-5, now I just do a shift or two over the weekend if I can be bothered to earn a few quid to buy essentials. The remainder of my week is free to idle.

Anon

DEAR IDLERS,

I work for one of the [..] rail maintenance companies, and our site inspections are pretty good work for an idler. By the time the track current is turned off and all of the paper work is sorted out, we normally get on the tracks and start work after 1am. We have to be off the tracks by about 4:30-5am before the current is turned back on. Hence most of the shifts are usually no longer than 3-4 hours. We still get paid for an eight hour shift though, and we get time-and-a-third for working at night.

Furthermore, because of massive amounts of bureaucracy, I reckon that about a quarter of all of our shifts are cancelled as soon as we turn up on site. So we get paid for doing a full eight hours' work for doing bugger all.

However, I reckon that the perfect job for an idler on the [...] is that of a "Protection Master". One of these chaps is required on site every time work is carried out on the tracks. They get paid an absolute fortune (they all drive Mercedes/BMWs) and their strenuous labour for the night goes as follows:

1. The track current is automatically turned off at about 1am.

2. The Protection Master places "Current Rail Indicator Device" (CRID) across the tracks.

3. The CRID confirms that the current has been turned off and it is safe to work on the tracks.

4. Protection Master gives the working team the nod to carry out their graft on the tracks, whilst the rest of the PM's shift comprises sitting around, reading The Sun and sleeping.
Anon

Have you got the perfect idler's job? Go to www.idler.co.uk/forum and let us know

SKIVERS AND

HEROES AND VILLAINS

MODERN DRUNKARD MAGAZINE

A superb website from the US, celebrating drinking and drunkenness with admirably amoral abandon. There is an essay on the wonderful Kingsley Amis, philosophical reflections on the nature of drinking in an article which asks the pertinent question, Are drunks hiding from reality, or changing it?, advice on "ditching the 9-5 grind" and a celebration of the pain of hangovers. Sterling work.

SLOWLONDON.COM (ABOVE)

This is a lovely gentle website with advice and reflection on enjoying life in the city. Although we would argue that it doesn't go quite far enough, running articles which recommend taking your full lunch hour when perhaps blowing your boss's brains out and running into the park with a bottle of champagne would be a more sensible option, it is nevertheless a useful corrective to the most damaging urban myth: the one that says busy-ness is good.

THE TARDIS STUDIOS

This underground labyrinth in Clerkenwell that was the Idler's playground for ten years until it closed recently. From the outside, it appears to be nothing more than a door in a wall but if you peer over the locked gates you will see the house plants now running riot, and if you listen closely, you can hear the fading echos of past good times.

NABOKOV'S SPEAK, MEMORY

"The curse of battle and toil leads man back to the boar, to the grunting beast's crazy obsession with the search for food. [...] Toilers of the world, disband! Old bucks are wrong. The world was made on a Sunday."

THE STRONG AND THE WEAK

Weakness is a fundamental building block of the universe. It is weak interaction that makes the sun burn. If matter were subject only to strong forces, stars would quickly fold in upon themselves. As the great space prophet Sun Ra once observed, "Power gets absorbed but weakness unleashed could destroy the whole earth".

MR ADDISON

The legendary and possibly apocryphal tax-ower who wrote a bitter letter to the Inland Revenue, accusing them of adding to the "endless stream of crapulent whining and panhandling vomited daily through the letterbox on to the doormat," from "pauper councils, Lombardy pirate banking houses and pissant gas-mongerers" and of "sucking the very marrows of those with nothing else to give". We need more of his type, heroic debunkers of the grinding bureaucracy of capitalism and state.

STRIVERS
OF THE IDLE UNIVERSE

CENTER FOR CONSUMER FREEDOM

A child prepares to lick a big ice cream but suddenly it is snatched from their grasps. A middle aged man relaxes with a beer only to have it dashed from his hand. Welcome to the shock tactics of this US pressure group, which is out to keep the world safe from the likes of Greenpeace and "anti-consumer gadflies trying to force an all-tofu diet on society". With its inflammatory rhetoric and funding from Big Food and (initially) Phillip Morris, the Center works hard to keep major corporations safe from litigation.

WIRELESS ROUTER

What's that, Mr Dixons? Do I want to have a wireless internet connection in my own home? And you say it is a lightening-fast, no-hassle set up? Here's my hundred quid. Oh no, is how the internet revolution ends - with a fat man crouched in his lounge, weeping over a little white box.

HAUTE COUTURE 1

High fashion begins by concealing the eyes, through hats or hair. The eyes give away our humanity, our commonality, where fashion bestows status by drawing lines between those in the know and outside of it. Evil starts with sunglasses.

HAUTE COUTURE 2

This is why fat men should never wear sunglasses. Humour is in the eyes, and if a large man is not jolly, why should we forgive his hoggishness? High fashion has netiher fat nor humour in it, just a pared-back, waspish cruelty.

INDIA: THE NEW CHINA

Just when you thought China was set to overtake US as the world's economic powerhouse India is now the nation being tipped to take its place. In the last twelve months the Indian Government has been courted by the world's leaders, feverishly squabbling over the potential profits to me made there. Mervyn King, head of the IMF, recently chose to make a speech in Delhi to point out how US and Euro-centric the outlook of the International Monetary Fund has become. And British Airways recently attributed a 4.7% rise in profits to the growth in business travel to India. Not bad for a country that secretly built nuclear weapons and still refuses to sign up to the Nuclear Non-Proliferation Treaty and was, as recently as 1998, having diplomatic and technology sanctions imposed on it by the US.

TONY HUSBAND'S JOKES PAGE

KNOWN TO HIS FRIENDS AS THE WORLD'S WORST JOKE TELLER,
TONY HUSBAND ASKS A FEW FAMOUS FACES FOR THEIR FAVOURITE GAGS.

Sam has been a wildlife biologist studying shrew behaviour for 25 years and is finally ready to sit down and write his doctoral dissertation. He finds the perfect writing spot, fifty acres of land in the Tennessee mountains as far from humanity as possible. Sam sees the postman once a week and gets groceries once a month. Otherwise it's total peace and quiet. After six months or so of almost total isolation, he's finishing dinner when someone knocks on his door. He opens it and there is a big, bearded man standing there.

"Name's Bo... Your neighbor from four miles away... Having a party Saturday... thought you'd like to come."

"Great," says Sam, "after six months out here I'm ready to meet some local folks. Thank you."

As Bo is leaving he stops, "Gotta warn you there's gonna be some drinkin'."

"Not a problem... after 25 years in the wildlife business, I can drink with the best of 'em."

Again, as he starts to leave Bo stops. "More 'n' likely gonna be some fightin' too."

Sam says, "Well, I get along with people. I'll be there. Thanks again."

Once again Bo turns from the door. "I've seen some wild sex at these parties, too."

"Now that's not a problem," says Sam, "I've been all alone for six months! I'll definitely be there... by the way, what should I wear?"

Bo stops in the door again and says, "Whatever you want, it's just gonna be the two of us".
[*Damien Hirst, Artist*]

Three dads sat in a pub, first dad says "My daughter's 14 and I found a pack of cigarettes in her room and I didn't know she smoked." Second dad says, "I found a half full bottle of gin in my daughters room, she is only 15 and I didn't know she drank."

The third dad says, "I found a pack of condoms in my daughter's room and she is sixteen and I didn't know she had a dick."
[*Sheila and Thomas Ravenscroft, Writers*]

A man wants to kill his wife so he hires a contract killer called Arty, the contract killer tells him he wants £10,000 for the job, the man says, "I've only got a pound on me, I'll give you the rest later." So the killer takes the money and goes to Tesco's where the man's wife is shopping. He sees her in the aisles, walks over and strangles her to death. As he is leaving an assistant shouts, "I saw that!" so to cover himself the man strangles him as well but he has been caught on CCTV and is captured outside by the police.

Next day the headline in the paper reads "Arty chokes 2 for a pound in Tescos."
[*Pete Boyle, Manchester United legend and cheerleader*]

My wife is like a knackered vacuum cleaner, she whines a lot and doesn't suck anymore.
[*Rob Spragg, lead singer, The Alabama 3*] ☺

THE FINE LINE BETWEEN

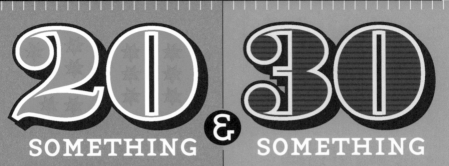

20 & 30

SOMETHING SOMETHING

ONE MINUTE YOU'RE LAUGHIN' AND PARTYIN',
THE NEXT JUST SPERMIN' AND EARNIN'

Dancing at nightclubs	You and your kid, covered in shit, screaming at each other
Bragging about your drug intake	Bragging about your bathroom
Playing board games in the pub	"I am bored of your games"
Arguing over the gastro-pub to host your hangover	One pint then you've got to be off
Hate listening to people talking about schools	Hating listening to yourself talking about schools
Reading novels with titles like My Knuckle Drug Diaries	Reading novels with titles like My Birkenstocks Are Broken
Can't get to sleep without a drink	Sleep?
Practising outrageous opinions	You no longer have anything to say
Three in a bed	Except one of them is a sleep-averse toddler
You will NEVER end up like them	Realising you were wrong when you said you will NEVER end up like them

LIFE IN THE SLOW LANE

John Legge hails the trusty milk float

A few days ago I was waiting for the bus into work. The rush hour was in full swing: great big saloons and 4x4s grumbled past, each with their single occupant. The traffic was moving slowly, and it was easy to see the tense frown on every face of every driver. I swear I could hear the gnashing of their teeth above the revving engines (I read a newspaper article recently describing a medical study which found western commuters to have higher stress levels than an airline pilot at take off, or a surgeon about to operate) .

Sitting there, mulling over the irony of the eager workers being forced to slow to a crawl for the one part of their busy day, it stuck me that we should be revelling in driving during the rush hour. You can't beat it, it is enforced idleness! However, this theory has flaws; cars are bad news. They pollute. They cost a fortune to run. They are an inefficient way of moving people (four seats and only one occupant). Then suddenly in the middle distance there appeared a convoy of white, swaying sedately along. The growl of internal combustion

was replaced by a soothing electric whine. A long column of empty milk floats sailed regally past, their working day behind them, cruising quietly, smoothly and smugly back to their depot.

Milk floats! It struck me that their slow speed wasn't a handicap in the rush hour, plus zero emissions! Arriving at work, I postponed starting the daily grind for a bit of research. A quick Google later I came across a website for milk float enthusiasts (http://www.milkfloats.org.uk/) I began to read and became excited. It turns out that second hand milk floats are cheap. Moreover, they are built to last—a strong metal chassis is required to carry the weight of the big lead acid battery packs. There isn't that much to go wrong with them; an electric float is just a frame with wheels, electric motor and some fairly basic wiring. Above all, there are a lot of them out there. People don't get milk delivered any more, they get it from the supermarket. The dairies are shrinking resulting in a glut of milk floats! The website said I could pick up a fairly basic used milk float for £500-1000. I looked on eBay where there where two being auctioned, both in working(ish) order. One had about two hours left on the auction, and the bidding had only reached £25. A pony for your own electric vehicle! And it got better. Electric floats don't need MOT testing. Although you need a Tax disc, it won't cost you anything. And they are exempt from the London congestion charge!

So how much would a float cost to run? If you give them their eight hour charge overnight (Using off-peak electricity) Mr Rees and Mr Fardell of Milk Float Corner website calculate about 1p per mile. The only serious expense is the batteries, which

JOHN LEGGE

FLOATING TO THE OFFICE... COULD MILK FLOATS BE THE NEW BUSES?

need replacing every ten years or so. A brand new set will typically set you back £1,800, but you can look for used ones.

So milk floats are cheap. Could you use one as transport? OK, most don't have cab doors, so they'd be drafty, and they only carry two people in the front, maybe three at a squeeze, but you could modify them; what about all that flatbed space on the rear? Why not fit a couple of old settees, and give your mates a lift into work? You could even pick up your fellow commuters on the way, pulling in at bus stops and offering free rides. Become knight errant and eco-warrior at the same time! It may be a bit chilly in winter with no heating and no sides on your "bus"—so why not take a big flask of hot chocolate and hand it round instead? Bring a little cheer and community (or commuterly) togeth-

erness to the start of the day. You could even go exotic and accessorise your float like the jeep buses in the Philippines or the decorated coaches in India, with a groovy paint job and elaborate drapes hanging from the roof. Personally, I'd keep my milk float simple—clean and white; I'd wear my Express Dairies logo with pride as I hummed along. What could be better? Start the electric revolution now! Don't let rush hour get you down—why crawl into work when you can float...? 🐌

MY FIRST JOB

MY FIRST SKIVE

Iain Aitch gets pissed on the job, aged 10

As a rule you should probably not accept job offers from men emerging from bushes in public parks in Margate, but that is how I was offered my first gainful employment back in 1979. I was ten years old. "How would you boys like to earn fifty-pee each?" asked my future boss.

There was really no need to ask what we would be required to do for the seven-sided coin that was coming our way.

"Follow me," said the boss.

He headed up the path and into the big house that sat on the other side of the topiary. When we reached the main body of the building it was clear that posh people had been having a party. Bottles were strewn all over the place and half-full glasses filled the foldaway tables. "OK," said the boss. "Just pick up these bottles, put them in those boxes and then put them out by the back door." He pointed.

"When do we get paid?" asked James.

"Well," said the boss. "You look trustworthy enough. So I'll give it to you now and I can go off and get on with the rest of my work."

He handed us each a shiny fifty-pence piece. There was really nothing more satisfying to hold in your hand at that time.

Larger and thicker than the current fifty-pence coin, this was a gateway to sweets, comics and fairground rides.

We filled boxes as fast as we could and made a game of it, as only young, un-jaded children can. When we were four or five full boxes into our task I picked up an interesting-looking bottle from the table that still had about one-third of its contents inside. It was champagne. My only knowledge of the stuff was that it was about as expensive as gold and was only to be drunk on special occasions.

I took a good swig. It didn't taste too great, but I tipped the bottle once more and glugged more of the outlandishly pricey booze. James came over and, finding more champagne dregs in a bottle on the same table, swigged, made a face and then swigged some more.

We swigged simultaneously. We swigged alternately. We tried to pour champagne into our mouth sangria-style, as we had seen on *The Generation Game*. We then discovered, somewhere in the bottom of those bottles, the spirit of idleness. We realized that as we had been paid and our boss didn't have a clue who we were then we could easily scarper with the job half-done. A fair day's pay for a sloppy half-hour's work.

We checked that the coast was clear and made for our bikes. We decided to split up. I cycled one way across the park whilst James headed off home in another, controlling his bike with one hand and holding on to his champagne with the other.

As coincidence would have it, another friend was later offered work by a man emerging from the bushes in a different local park, these handy shrubs obviously operating something like an unofficial Job Centre in Margate.

The man asked my friend to piss on him while he lay down on the grass. ☺

THE TRUTH ABOUT... EDUCATION

SCHOOL'S OUT

Brian Dean says children are not legally required to go to school

While the press focus on exams and school performance, children are becoming targets of the government's war on non-conformity. Crackdowns on truants and unruly pupils don't, however, alter the fact that school is optional.

CRACKDOWNS ON YOUTH

THE POLICE have powers (Crime & Disorder Act 1998) to remove children playing truant from public places. Parents of truants face fines or jail—11,500 parents have been placed on a "Fast Track to Prosecution". The government wants to go even further, according to *The Independent*: "Ministers want to make it an offence to allow children to roam unsupervised in a public place."

National "truancy sweeps" were introduced in 2002—the latest one stopped 12,808 children over a three-week period, but more than half of those stopped had a valid reason for being out of school. Over 16,000 hours of police time are spent annually on truancy sweeps. To convince the public of the seriousness of the issue, the Department for Education and Skills (DfES) quotes statistics linking truancy to crime. But government guidelines define lateness as a category of truancy, and the Guardian reports that some truancy sweeps have been conducted outside school gates, with late-arriving pupils being recorded as truants. Does lack of punctuality lead to a life of crime?

In some cases the bureaucratic control-freakery gets even weirder. The *Manchester Evening News* reported a case of a woman placed under curfew and electronically tagged after her children regularly bunked off school. And, demonstrating insight into child psychology, The London Borough of Kingston is resurrecting a Victorian practice of awarding medals to children with 100% school attendance records. Meanwhile, over two thousand parents of truants have been forced to sign "parenting contracts" to improve their child's attendance, and a government task-force recently called for a "national behaviour charter".

Since 1998 the government has spent nearly £1 billion on "tough" measures to tackle truancy, but the National Audit Office reported (in February 2005) that the truancy rate remained unchanged between 1998 and 2004. The government responded to this report of failure by promising a "tougher approach".

JOHN MIERS

PARENTS AREN'T LEGALLY REQUIRED TO SEND THEIR CHILDREN TO SCHOOL

SCHOOL IS OPTIONAL

PARENTS AREN'T legally required to send their children to school. According to section 7 of the 1996 Education Act, children must receive "suitable" education "at a school or otherwise". Parents don't need permission to educate their kids "otherwise". If a child is already registered at a school, the parents can simply notify the head teacher of their wish to educate "otherwise". Children who are deregistered from school in this way are, in theory, free from the harassment of truancy sweeps.

Tens of thousands of UK children have an education based at home. Local Education Authorities (LEAs) can do nothing about it except request evidence that a child is receiving "suitable" education. They can't prescribe how that evidence is to be presented nor demand to enter parents' homes.

The law requires an education suitable to a child's "age, ability, and aptitude", but there are no rules dictating what a child must learn. There's no obligation, for example, to teach them "core subjects" such as Maths and English. In an appeal case at Worcester Crown Court in 1981, the judge defined a "suitable education" as one which prepares children for "life in modern civilized society" and which enables them to "achieve their full potential".

In another case, reported by *The Times*, Mr Justice Woolf held that: "Education is 'suitable' if it primarily equips a child for life within the community of which he is a member, rather than the way of life in the country as a whole, as long as it does not foreclose the child's options in later years to adopt some other form of life if he wishes to do so."

FLEXI-SCHOOL

THE 1996 EDUCATION ACT requires that children receive a "full-time" education, but it doesn't define "full-time". With no legal obligation to observe school hours, days or terms, the phrase "full-time" is open to interpretation—if not entirely irrelevant—in school-free contexts.

In fact, children can legally attend school on a part-time, flexible basis. As the website flexischooling.info puts it, "school becomes one of many resources, such as libraries, computers, television, etc, to be used when the child and the parents choose, according to a contract between them and the local school." Any school may accommodate flexi-schooling, but schools are entitled to refuse it on arbitrary grounds, including the fear that it might start a trend. LEAs can advise schools about flexi-schooling, but can't impose their view.

CONFORMITY COPS

DESPITE THE INCREASING POPULARITY of flexi-school and non-school education, government agencies sometimes associate these options with social isolation, exclusion and "children at risk".

Many parents of children who are unhappy at school remain unaware of their legal right to educate at home. In a May 2003 parliamentary debate (the first ever on the subject of home education), John Randall MP mentioned cases in which education officials "encouraged" parents to return their near-suicidal children to school, rather than pro-vide information on the legal alternatives. He also mentions cases where "parents have willingly gone to jail, rather than send a school-phobic child to school", adding, "it seems outrageous that—despite months of meetings and discussions with officials—in many cases, parents are not even informed about the option to deregister their child and home educate."

SOCIALIZATION

Home-learning groups report that "socialization" is the issue most often raised by enquirers. Many people fear that without school kids will have no friends and become socially inept. This appears similar to the politicians' fear that people without jobs become socially isolated. Both fears seem to arise from the bizarre notion that friends are found only in state—or corporate-controlled environ-ments. Or that classrooms and offices provide the best models for social harmony. Schools, like most workplaces, provide a type of socialization that is imposed and confined—it resembles prison. It's a strange logic that equates freedom from confine-ment with isolation.

In November 2001, the *Daily Mail* printed a letter from a home-educated 15 year-old girl addressing the socialization issue: "Away from the cliquey environment of the classroom, I've been able to build friendships from choice rather than proximity and I'm free to go out without worrying about homework [...] Timetables and age-segregation are forms of crowd control and nothing to do with edu-cation. Away from the crowds, real learning can begin."

SCHOOL AND JOBS

The regimented nature of school trains the young to accept regimented employment. How else can society prepare children for an adult life of daily confinement performing boring tasks and following orders? Ever since 1833, when state-funded edu-cation was introduced, schools have mass-pro-duced what society needs: relatively docile, compli-ant young citizens ready to slot straight into tedious jobs.

The New Labour government has tried to make this process more efficient with a managerial approach of goals, targets, benchmarks and statistical appraisals. The bottom line for schools and pupils is measure-ment of performance. Perfect preparation for today's dynamic corporate environment.

School-free education gives children a taste of freedom and self-reliance, remote from per-formance-obsessed authorities. No need to ask permission for the toilet, no pressure to con-form. If it catches on, it might result in fewer young people accepting the role of wage slave. It must seem like a dangerous trend to those responsible for running the national economy. ◉

**Brian Dean runs
anxietyculture.com**

Sources, respectively: "Fast Track to Prosecution" from BBC news online, 6/9/05; Independent, 22/10/05; DfES figures for March 2005 truancy sweeps; "16,000 hours" from study by Action on Rights for Children; Guardian, 6/9/05; Manchester Online, 29/4/05; BBC news, 26/9/05; £885m spent tackling truancy 1998-2004 according to National Audit Office press release, 4/2/05; National Audit Office report, 'Improving school atten-dance in England', February 2005; Court cases cited by Education Oth-erwise; Mr Justice Woolf quote from Times, 12/4/85; John Randall quotes from Hansard, 13/5/03; Daily Mail let-ters page, 9/11/01)

SHOW US YOUR BUM

Sarah Janes on getting your kit off

There are two absolute truths in my world. One is that having a laugh with your mates is the greatest fun in the world! And the second is that life gets much more interesting if, upon waking, you look into the sky and screech—"MORNING LORD! WHAT HAVE YOU GOT FOR ME TODAY?" The world is full of limitless fun and adventure. When you are a kid, you really understand this. You feel it. Love equals joy and you are blissfully unselfconscious and full of wonderment and beauty. It should be every human's life work to maintain a childish outlook.

A few months ago my five year old nephew, then four, listened to music through headphones for the first time ever. To see his enraptured face, tears twinkling in the corners of his eyes, his perfect body glowing with pleasure, was a sight I will never forget. My whole family sat and watched as he trembled with glee. Grinning and dancing and unbuttoning his shirt and wriggling out of his trousers until he was dancing in his pants and then, frolicking naked, like a desperately happy little animal.

The rest of my family tried to get him to put his clothes back on, but I completely understood how he felt and was so happy for him to be young and lovely and

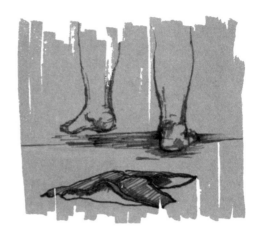

CHLOE KING

aching with delight. He wiggled his bare bottom at us and then, not feeling sufficiently exposed—perhaps not making sufficient intimate contact with every joy filled particle of air—he pulled apart his bum cheeks and showed us his arsehole.

My mum and dad said—"that's enough now Jack. That's not funny" but Jack looked at me and said—"funny?" and I said—"that's the funniest thing I've ever seen in my life, that is brilliant!" And I cried with laughter. My mum and dad said—"don't encourage him" (thus encapsulating everything that is wrong with modern society.)

Every now and again I feel just like Jack did that day. Sometimes, social programming stops me from taking off all my clothes in front of rooms full of people. Sometimes, the seductive qualities of expensive booze positively encourage it. Public nakedness is never purer than when you are a kid and exposure is something distinctly unsleazy, unfrowned upon, unregrettable and doesn't tend to involve having to get the morning after pill. ◉

GOTH MUM!

A GRIMM FAIRYTALE

LAZY HEINZ

The Brothers Grimm relate a blissfully moral-free tale of man and wife

Heinz was lazy, and although he had nothing else to do but drive his goat out to the pasture every day, he nevertheless groaned every evening when he returned home after each day's work.

"It is in truth a heavy burden," he said, "and a tiresome job, to drive such a goat out to the field until late in the autumn. If I could only lie down and sleep at it! But no, I must keep my eyes open so it won't damage the young trees, or force its way through the hedge into a garden, or even run away altogether. How can I get some rest and enjoy life?"

He sat down, collected his thoughts, and considered how he could lift the burden of toil from his shoulders. For a long time his thoughts led to nothing, but suddenly it was as if scales were removed from his eyes.

"I know what I will do," he said. "I will marry Fat Trina. She too has a goat, and she can drive mine out with hers, and then I shall no longer have to torment myself."

So Heinz got up, set his weary legs into motion, and walked across the street, for it was no further than that, to where Fat Trina's parents lived, and asked for the hand in marriage of their daughter.

Her parents did not think about it for long. "Birds of a feather, flock together," they thought, and gave their consent.

So Fat Trina became Heinz's wife, and drove out both of the goats. Heinz now enjoyed life, having no work to rest from, but his own laziness.

He went out with her only now and then, saying, "I'm doing this so that afterwards I will enjoy resting more. Otherwise I shall lose all feeling for it."

However, Fat Trina was no less lazy.

"Dear Heinz," she said one day, "why should we make our lives so miserable, ruining the best days of our youth, when there is no need for it? The two goats disturb our best sleep every morning with their bleating. Wouldn't it be better for us to give them to our neighbour, who will give us a beehive for them? We will put the beehive in a sunny place behind the house, and then not give it any more thought. Bees do not have to be taken care of, nor driven into the field. They fly out and find their way home again by themselves, and they collect honey without any effort at all on our part."

"You have spoken like a sensible woman," replied Heinz. "We will carry out your proposal without delay. And furthermore, honey tastes better and is more nourishing than goat's milk, and it keeps longer too."

The neighbour willingly gave them a beehive for the two goats. The bees flew tirelessly in and out from early morning until late evening, filling the hive with the best honey. Thus, come autumn, Heinz was able to take out a whole jugful.

They placed the jug on a shelf on their bedroom

wall. Fearing that it might be stolen, or that the mice might get into it, Trina brought in a stout hazel stick and put it beside her bed, so that she would be able to reach it without having to get up, and then from her place in bed drive away the uninvited guests.

Lazy Heinz did not like to get out of bed before noon. "He who rises early," he would say, "wastes his wealth."

One morning when he was still lying in the feathers in broad daylight, resting from his long sleep, he said to his wife, "Women are fond of sweets, and you have been snacking on the honey. It would be better for us to exchange it for a goose with a young gosling, before you eat it all up."

"But not before we have a child to take care of them," replied Trina. "Am I to torment myself with the young geese, wasting all my energy on them for no reason?"

"Do you think," said Heinz, "that the boy will tend geese? Nowadays children no longer obey. They do just as they please, because they think that they are smarter than their parents."

"Oh," replied Trina, "he will get it if he does not do what I say. I will take a stick and tan his hide with more blows than can be counted."

"See here, Heinz," she shouted in her fervor, seizing the stick that she intended to use to drive away the mice. "See here! This is how I will beat him."

JACOB AND WILLHELM GRIMM

She struck forth, unfortunately hitting the jug of honey above the bed. The jug struck against the wall and fell down in pieces. The fine honey flowed out onto the floor.

"There lies the goose with the young gosling," said Heinz. "And they do not need to be tended. But it is lucky that the jug did not fall on my head. We have every reason to be satisfied with our fate."

Then noticing that there was still some honey in one of the pieces of the jug, he reached out for it, saying quite happily, "Wife, let us enjoy the leftovers, and then we will rest a little from the fright we have had. What does it matter if we get up a little later than usual? The day will be long enough."

"Yes," answered Trina, "there is always time enough. You know, the snail was once invited to a wedding and started on his way, but arrived at the child's baptism. In front of the house it fell over the fence, and said, 'Haste makes waste.'" 🐌

THE WIT AND WISDOM OF

WILLIAM
DONALDSON (1935-2005)

Paul Hamilton on a moral free spirit

"The salient features about me are laziness, self-indulgence and sex addiction. I'm genuinely shocked by my own behaviour."

Producer, pimp and prankster *par excellence* William Donaldson lived such a turbulent life—inheriting £175,000 and a 30-room country mansion before he was 25, a destitute beachcomber fifteen years later, a crack cocaine addict in his sixties— that were he a fictional character you wouldn't believe it. His character Henry Root was the right-wing, educated-in-the-University-of-Life, wildly patriotic self-made humbug, a Pooter for the Thatcher Years, and Donaldson's subversive weapon to wield against intellectually inflexible politicians, vanity-stricken celebrities and petit-bourgeoise conservative values. Donaldson, alarmingly, had little in the way of scruples: A former wife, Claire Gordon, was understandably mortified to discover that Donaldson had sent sex contact magazines pornographic photographs of her in exchange for publicity for her get-fit video. Never overly keen on rubbernecked boozery, he nonetheless retained his deep affection for hard and dangerous drugs till the end of his life, including the date rape drug Rohypnol, of which he had one complaint: "The trouble is it wipes your memory. You have to video yourself to appreciate just what a good time you had." Preferring the comparatively unpretentious company of drug dealers and prostitutes to the bullshit inanities of showbiz practitioners it was perhaps inevitable that in 1970 Donaldson made the papers under the headline CANNABIS CASE IMPRESSARIO FINED. WHEN CAUTIONED THE ACCUSED ASKED THE ARRESTING OFFICER, "HAVEN'T I SEEN YOU AT ONE OF MY POT PARTIES?" (His sexual appetites were maybe less exotic than most, but whereas other people keep zip-lipped about their respective kinky peccadilloes, Donaldson was refreshingly outspoken: "Who wouldn't want a naked woman dancing round their front room? Or am I being infantile?" he wondered in 2002.)

Self-effacing, Donaldson professed no great gifts as a writer ("It's all about showing off, it's not serious. It's why my journalism was so rubbish") but as a wit and a whizz he has few equals. Here is a selection from four of his very many books. *Both The Ladies And The Gentlemen* is his autobiography of his time as the pimp—or ponce— to his former secretary-turned-prostitute. "The Big One, The Black One, The Fat One And The Other One." The other titles find Donaldson deep-Rooted. Should you discover yourself assenting with the uninformed babblings of the former wet fish merchant, then you're definitely batting for the wrong team in Donaldson's view.

. . .

IF I HAD a pound for every occasion that someone has told me that watching television is a waste of time, I'd be a rich man. And if it is a waste of time, how are we to describe the balls-aching tedium of being trapped in a corner of a strange room by a copywriter one has never previously met or by a pub actor with a grudge? So Emma Jane went [to the dinner party] on her own, and came back after an hour looking virtuous. "Did you enjoy yourself?" I asked. "Not really," she said, "but one ought to go out." I don't understand this at all.

. . .

In my day, the fuzz wouldn't have indulged in anything so time-consuming or clumsy as a search for evidence; more sensibly, they brought it with them. When they did this to me, I wasn't too bothered. They seemed to me to be nice enough fellows who simply had this one behavioural tic—a compulsion to plant pot on members of the laity whose lifestyle they thought might be to their taste. How else, after all, are lowly detectives going to get in to the houses of their betters, save by coming through the front door with a search warrant in one hand and an ounce of pot in the other which, in the attendant confusion, they conjure from nowhere with the aplomb of Channing Pollock plucking doves out of thin air?

. . .

What of the role of ponce? In many ways it ought to be one of the most desirable. It has little public status and

as a convenient label at a cocktail party it's pretty much a non-starter. It's self-evident that the only happy horses in the Grand National are those whose jockeys have fallen off. Beaming from ear to ear, they gambol around the course, ogling their friends in the stand and generally being a bloody nuisance to those horses

still bent on winning. No doubt they get a bollocking on their return to the stables for failing to take the outing seriously, but this is a price they're probably prepared to pay. Ponces, similarly shed of their obligations, present the same carefree demeanour to the world. Thanks to this role, the surface facts of my life are better than they've ever been. The grub's good; there are two colour television sets; cash is distributed like Monopoly money; nobody harasses me; I can get all the culture I need from the local library; sensual stimulation is more available than it should be to an old fart; for the first time in my life I have a job that doesn't require me to traffic with unacceptable people. I have no problems—and this is precisely what's wrong. I accept the theory that it's the innate need to solve problems that gets us from pillar to post, and a ponce's problems are simply not interesting enough.

· · ·

THE MAD HARRY TELEPHONE JAPE: This involves six people taking it in turns to ring up a complete stranger over a period of two hours, asking to speak to Mad Harry. By the sixth call the total stranger has become hysterically tired of saying he's never heard of such a person. "Well, tell him I rang," says each prankster, leaving a different name. Then the last person rings and says, "It's

Mad Harry here. Are there any messages for me?" and the total stranger's brain drops out. (Tremendous fun.)

· · ·

The fact is, I hadn't much enjoyed the shoot; more accurately, I hadn't enjoyed it at all. What had surprised me most, I think, was that everyone else involved seemed to look on it as work—evidence of this being that once a week we were given a day off.

The trick is, as I see it, is to get paid for what you do anyway and, if you can't get that organised, you might as well sit on a beach with corks in your hat. Either way, what's the point of a day off? I've never done a day's work in my life (except when I inadvertently did the same day twice at Ogilvy & Mather), and, equally, have never had a day off.

There had, too, been a telling incident in Paris. A street drunk [...] kept wandering into the action, giving his opinion on how the scene might be better directed and offering [director] Mark Chapman a swig from his bottle of red wine. Chapman finally blew up with an exasperated "not while I'm working!", obviously expecting "working" to have the effect on the drunk of garlic on a vampire. The drunk rocked with laughter, and so did I. Why, I wondered, hadn't Chapman taken a swig or, at least, said "not while I'm amusing myself making silly movies"? This isn't for me, I thought.

. . .

AESTHETICS: Art for art's sake. "You can't judge a book by its contents, that's what I always say." See Keats, The Melancholy Mr.

CRISIS, IDENTITY: Youngsters these days are much afflicted by so-called identity crises. "I'm off to India to get my head together. I don't know who I am." Identity crises were unheard of before the discontinuation of National Service. See Service, National; and Lulu.

FERRY, BRIAN [sic] (b.1948): Pop singer. The triumph of artifice. What he is about is that he isn't about anything.

HEROIN: One shot and you're a dead man. A recent survey showed that 97.8 per cent of all heroin users had at some time in their lives experimented with so-called pot. Need anything more be said? "My round, is it?"

KEITH, PENELOPE (b.1930): The funniest woman who ever lived. "She could make me roar with laughter just reciting the electoral register!" In an interview be sure to ask her whether she's as frightful in real life as Margot in The Good Life.

LABOUR: Refer to the dignity of labour. No one knows what it is.

LOBBY, THE ANTI-SMOKING: Admirable in theory, but made up —all too predictably—of the same vociferous do-gooders who advocate the liberalization of cannabis, which not only pits the lungs but addles the brain, causes men to grow breasts and destroys the family. "The upshot? Excreta through the letter-box! Mark my words. Care for another?"

OLDS, NINETY-SIX-YEAR: Always "sprightly".

OPERA: See Rates, Art On The.

OPINIONS, LEFT-WING: Always "half-baked".

PAYER, THE TAX: Always "long-suffering". "Someone has to pay. And I know who. The long-suffering tax payer. That's you and me."

REVOLUTIONARIES: Revolutionaries are the last people to realize when, through age and status, they themselves have become conservatives.

RING, THE BOXING: The loneliest place in the world. You can run but you can't hide.

SEX, PROMISCUOUS: Always "joyless". A sure sign of depression. A cry for help.

STRIKERS, HUNGER: They choose to die, but their victims had no choice. "That's what I always say."

TESTS, INTELLIGENCE: Mistrust them. Intelligence is culturally relative. If a Hottentot set an intelligence test how many Oxbridge philosophers would pass?

VICIOUS, SID (1959-1980 [sic]): When he and his girlfriend Nancy Spungen met up after a lengthy separation they were so pleased to see each other that they had a bottle-fight. In a humorous column, "Mr Sidney Vicious".

VIOLENCE, RAPE AND: When a culture encourages people to think and act on a basis of "I want it now", it inevitably leads, via colour supplement values, to rape and violence.

WALES: A history of marvellous stories, none of them true. History with a wry smile.

WARD, STEPHEN (1910-1963): Ponce to the Establishment or sacrificial goat? The debate continues, but surely we don't need to be reminded yet again that Jack Profumo copulated with a tart, deceived his wife— the lovely and gracious Valerie Hobson—endangered the security of the State and lied to the House of Commons? He has paid his debt to society and should now be left in peace. ☙

Further reading:
Brewer's Rogues, Villains And Eccentrics An A-Z Of Roguish Britons Through The Ages (2002).

k1d5-eh?

About your darling offspring

This combined application form for *Child Benefit* and the *Tag Card – The New Identity Card for Kids Who Know What's Good For Them*™ – must be completed in magenta ink by a parent, guardian, scout leader, brown owl or borstal line manager in block capitals with a Home Office approved pen, such as the *Blunkliner Elite 1984*.

Your child's name in full

If your child is royal, has fifteen middle names and qualifies for a widescreen birth certificate, you may continue on a separate scroll of vellum, if Your Fecund Majesty Pleases.

How old is he/she/it?

0-2 Please wipe the toxic compound of chicken gack and infant snot from your lapels before filling in the rest of this form.

3-10 Please tell us all about your child's frankly unnatural obsession with horses, hamsters or Jesus.

11-18 Apply for your child's Ford Fiesta hotwiring kit and ASBO Gift Vouchers straight away.

Are you really the biological parent?
We need to ask you this in order
to cause as much deep offence as
possible.

Yes Please provide proof such as a matching DNA profile or the sworn affidavit of a senior government minister that did not sleep with your partner.

No Please answer the following question.

Your relationship to child expressed in pseudo-legalese latin terminology

Pater/mater   In loco parentis   Ingloriaestefan   Alfrescopanettoné

Do not write or mark below this line or you will be sent to stand in the Naughty Corner.

Official Use Only

Action to be taken

Go to lunch   Issue excuse   Moan about line manager

Leave behind radiator   Ignore completely   Escalate

IAN VINCE

About their funny little ways

Are any of your children feral?
By feral, we mean "located on a street corner and/or bus shelter and in possession of an alcopop, a 50 Cent CD or a bicycle with absurdly small wheels".

Yes ☐ I agree to enrol them forthwith into a tough-love reality TV programme where their serious behavioural problems can be channelled into entertaining the fat, ugly, braying masses.

No ☐ My children have been gently thwarted from birth and will therefore only require serious psychotherapy after they have left home.

How do you discipline your child?
For more information on disciplining your child, talk to friends who have no children but read the Daily Mail and bloody-well know everything.

☐ As a liberal parent I know that only careful negotiation and patient reasoning will lead to the return of the unmarked bank notes and the safe release of all the hostages.

☐ My child may not be negotiated or reasoned with without the aid of Cold War-era mind games and/or quantities of Green Kryptonite.

How does your child protect and manage their personal space?

☐ My adolescent daughter defends her personal space by existing in a noxious cloud of synthesized pink gases and scowling bitchiness.

☐ My teenage son is propagating a black hole-based universe where only death metal, but no light, can enter or escape the event horizon formed by the boundary of his hooded top.

Declaration
I declare that I have done my best with the little shit(s), but it's a thankless task and I still believe that my parents did it all wrong.

Signed

GCSE Skills Assessment Area

1	2		4	5	6

Single line Suduko.
Rating: Unduly prescriptive

Tutorial Assessment Guidelines

- Examiners are reminded that applications should be marked for presentation *and* comprehension.
- The value of your child may go down as well as up.

IAN VINCE

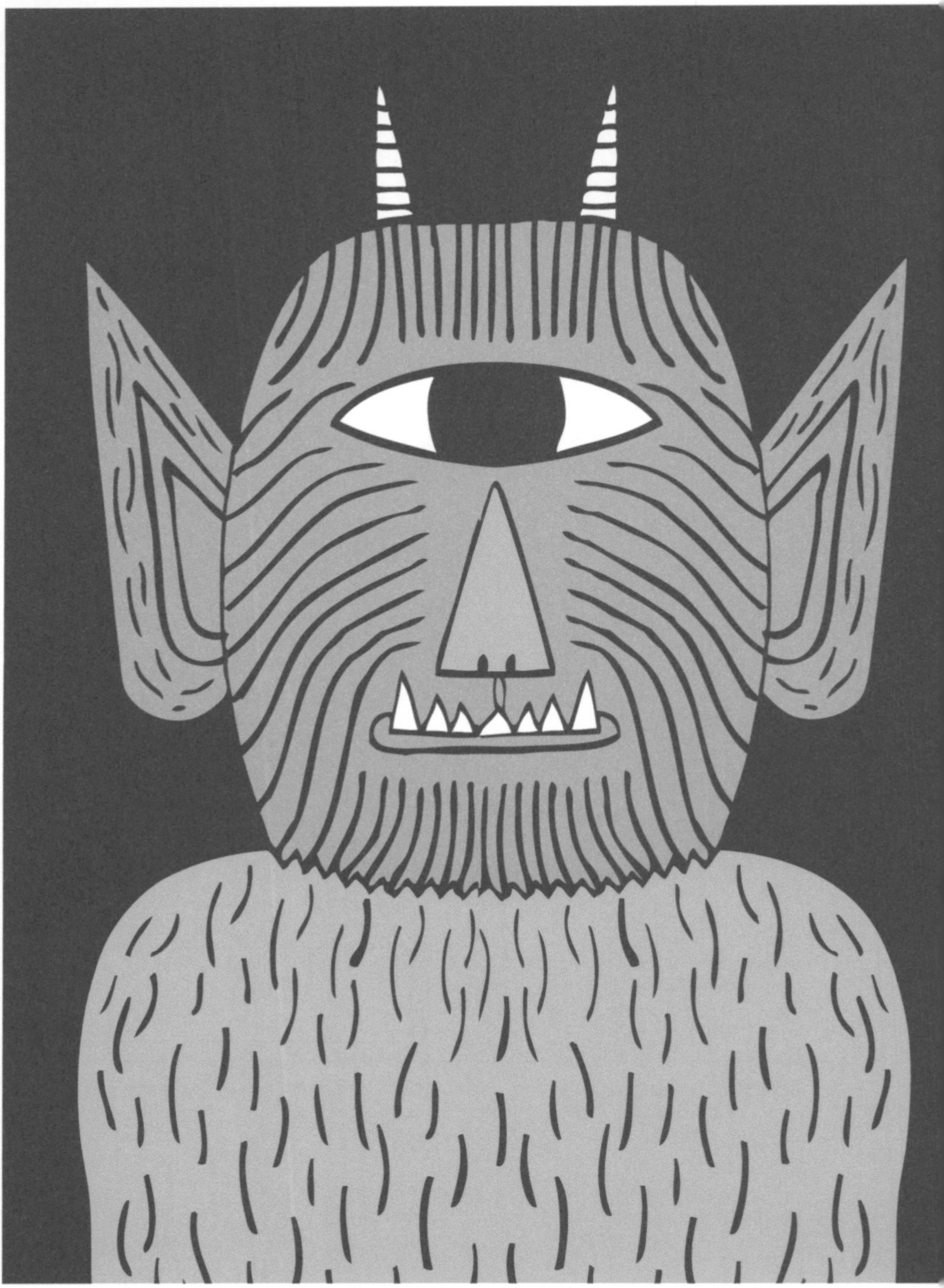

A MANIFESTO

Billy Childish on creative freedom

Creativity is not originality, originality is God.

...

Creativity is what brings man closer to God.

...

Creativity is the willingness to play.

...

Children are expert at play and remain so up until they are taught not to play.

...

An infant school classroom of twenty children has twenty children who are unafraid to draw, play and express themselves.

...

A junior school classroom of thirty children has ten children who are unafraid to draw, play and express themselves.

...

A secondary school of 700 children has five children who are unafraid to draw, play and express themselves.
But don't worry, art school is there waiting to smash the survivors.

...

An art school of 700 students has two students who are unafraid to draw, play and express themselves. One of them will leave and the other will be expelled.

...

The adult who is not in touch with his creativity and inherent childishness is not an adult but a stunted child.

...

The world of grown ups is crammed to the lid with stunted children.

...

This is why we have a lack of beauty in art, architecture and our lives are ruled by fear and greed.

...

As long as we judge art and life by the dictates of fashion and commerce we will be like vile Cyclops.

...

To become free we could do as Jesus Christ suggested and become more like children again.

...

The most creative man alive draws what he loves with a bit of burnt stick then chucks on some powder paints and smiles at his own stupidity.

MARCUS OAKLEY

CRAP HOLIDAYS

SAILING IN GREECE

I was only fifteen and it was my first proper foreign holiday so naturally I was very excited. So were my parents, both of whom had just passed the sailing course that they needed to have completed in order to hire the boat in the first place. Quite what we would have done if they'd failed I have no idea. If only we'd been lucky enough to find out.

The holiday consisted of renting a boat for a fortnight as part of a flotilla sailing around the Greek Islands. You had the choice of following everyone else or going off and doing your own thing. My parents decided we should go off and do our own thing. With a couple they'd just met from Nottingham called Jason and Ange. I wanted to follow Claire and Robert from Liverpool and their beautiful daughter Jenny. But we didn't.

I got sun burnt on the second day, forgetting that you don't really feel your skin blistering in the light mediterranean breeze. I spent the rest of the holiday dowsed in after-sun and covered up by a baggy tracksuit. I was unable to go out in the sun, swim or do anything during daylight hours. If only the same could be said for Jason and Ange.

Jason and Ange turned out to be naturists. This was quite off-putting for everyone else on the flotilla, who subsequently avoided us like the plague. Jason was hung like a rhinoceros and Ange was shaved bare. Not the kind of accompaniment a virgin fifteen-year-old needs on holiday but soon, staggeringly, things got worse. After two days Jason and Ange had persuaded my parents to become naturists too. Embarrassment isn't the word. Especially when Claire and Robert from Liverpool were about to moor alongside us. My nude mum, bent over a coil of rope shouted, "Oh David, look it's Jenny!" at which point Claire and Robert realised both my parents were naked and promptly sailed off again. Then we got stuck in a storm. Being on a sailing boat in a storm with naked, and now arguing parents, was the last straw. After that I vowed I never to go on a family holiday ever again... ◉ **David Le Tissier**

SON - A HOLIDAY IS A LOT LIKE LIFE. THERES A BLACK EMPTY NOTHINGNESS BEFORE IT, AND THERES A DEATH-LIKE BLACK EMPTY NOTHINGNESS AFTER IT

GWYN

THREE FEET HIGH

Ava Moore wants it now

Look, I've made it quite clear—I don't want to go in the water, I just want a lollipop from the machine at the swimming pool. Surely that's not too much to ask, is it? Just drive me to the swimming pool—come on it won't take long. And... I must have that towel... I mean, I simply must have it—the one with the whale on it—it's essential... yes, I know I've got other towels, but they're not the same. It matches the flannel Nanny gave me when I was sick in the car... If you give me that towel, I'll give you ten kisses... a hundred kisses. I'm holding it tightly and I'm not putting it down... ow, you're hurting me. If you give me that towel, I'll say good morning at school... yes of course it's a promise—if it wasn't for you I wouldn't be so shy would I, scabby pants? Anyway, I'm not being shy, I'm just being difficult.

Stop! Turn around—I want to show you something. I want to buy it. What do you mean I haven't got any money? I don't need any—I've got you. *Poppy Cat's Christmas Book.* I know it's not Christmas. It's not a Christmas book—whatever gave you that idea? No, I'm not leaving this shop without it... unthinkable. I'll say good afternoon to my teacher... We'd better hide it though. I know there are lots of

ARE YOU STUPID, DADDY?

them, but this is my one... put it up here where no one will see.

I'm not eating that sandwich until you've taken the lettuce out. I know I said I loved lettuce—that was then, this is now. Well... thirty seconds *is* a long time. Well...I don't like lettuce. No you can't have it, it's for the rabbits... which rabbits? Any rabbits. No, I won't eat crusts, I don't want curly hair. Can you buy me a lollipop—the heart shaped one? But I'm hungry. I might have asked for tuna sandwiches, but what I really meant was the heart shaped lollipops next to them. I must have a straw... and some sticks to put in it. What do you mean what is this? Are you stupid? It's a nose bridge of course, what does it look like? Really daddy, you're a bit slow sometimes. ☺

OUT OF THE DARKNESS

Frankie Poullain is in exile

AMORAL, WHIMSICAL, LAZY

Yes, I am Frankie Poullain. Perhaps you'll remember me for slagging off Keane. Perhaps for falling out with my glamorous assistant Justin Hawkins. Perhaps for allegedly fishing and growing vegetables in the grounds of my old French Chateau. Perhaps for the bandana 'n' tache combo. Perhaps even for lines like: "When you're climbing a mountain you don't stop halfway and start sucking your own cock." Other triggers could include 118 118, Ming The Merciless or *Zoolander*.

In an era of reality TV saturation I suppose I could propose a "Frankie Panky", a "Poullain Power" or even a "Frankie Goes To Bollywood", assuming anyone, including myself, actually gave a monkeys.

"Who is he and what the fuck is he on about?" you're probably thinking. OK, bear with me if you will ...

It seems only last week that the lead singer of an infamous cock rock band (OK, The Darkness) outlined his vision of an updated *Bullseye* for today's newly reinvigorated darts public. The proposed programme would be a pro-celeb affair called *Fame On*, thereby ingeniously tweaking the term "Game On". Not bad at all I thought. This got me thinking about a less dumbed down but similarly retro weekly half hour show. Ideally it would combine the "loose cannon geek in a tank top" factor of Bamber Gascoigne era *University Challenge* and the lewd utter nonsense of *Topless Darts*, laced with a sprinkling of *Wife Swap* for good measure.

A pair of contestants, preferably from opposite ends of the social, cultural and geographical divide, would argue the toss on a given contentious topic. In the midst of this a lie detector would administer electric shocks directly to the temple area—as a way of policing the porky pie factor you understand. But the actual aim would be to verbally trump or whammy an opponent.

Five whammies and you're out! It wouldn't necessarily have to take place in a TV studio, we could be looking at the more traditional battlefields: a dole office queue, by the kitchen sink or even outdoor at a bus stop. Any attempt at physical contact or intimidation would be punishable by the victim selecting an item of the offender's clothing to be discarded. Any item. The best way to deal with bullies, surely?

The points master would naturally have to be someone schooled in LIFE. Meaning not your stereotypical BBC2 Oxbridge in-house smarmathon. So, no Stephen Fry, Angus Deayton or Ian Hislop. Garth Crooks from *Football Focus* fame would be my personal choice—the guy is a bona fide twenty-four carrot demented ENIGMA, every Saturday lunchtime somehow investing the humdrum Sven Goran Eriksson with the mystifying qualities of a Stephen Hawking—there's something admirable about that surely? If you haven't heard of him (any ladies out there, go on, google him) worry not—I don't know how and I don't know when, but I do know that Garth Crooks is destined for the front pages. Call it "free-male" intuition if you like. Chris Eubank's credentials (monocle, lisp, jodhpurs, hard as fuck) should also be taken into consideration.

So, back to the show and now

I DO NOT ALLOW FINANCIAL PRESSURES, SOCIAL MORES, RESPONSIBILITIES OR CONVENTIONAL WISDOM TO DICTATE MY LIFESTYLE

it's all about the title. Something refreshingly snappy and attention grabbing with just a hint of the everyday... it's just GOT to be: "MASTER DEBATE 2006". The Master Debater Champions of England, Scotland, Wales and Northern Ireland would then play off for the Great British Master Debater's Goblet.

I suppose at this point I'm expected to delve into Darkness anecdote territory. Thing is, there's the small matter of upcoming legal issues and a probable court case. Perhaps myself and Justin should simply go ahead and take a wanker detector test? Admittedly that'd be a lot of work for the machine but he WOULD struggle definitely.... That was a bit childish wasn't it? READ MY LIPS: it—will—all—come—out—in—the—wash. Let's just hope the colours don't run! Perhaps a colder rinse would be best, say 30 degrees centigrade?

Epilogue: I am a lazy twat who spent years on the dole gazing adoringly at my own navel. I now use the newfound relative wealth to tickle my fancies. I suppose you'd describe me as a restlessly curious yet oddly detached and occasionally inert beast. On good days it's "a Moveable Feast". I do not allow financial pressures, social mores, personal responsibilities or the scourge that is conventional wisdom to dictate my lifestyle, preferring instead to be guided by whims, nay, interests of which I have a veritable banquet. So, I'm an idler, right? 🐌

FRATRICIDE

Jamie Dwelley indulges murderous impulses. Illustration by Gwyn

I recall, quite vividly, thinking, "what the fuck is that?" when my sister came home for the first time.

I was nearly three. I was furious; this tiny pink creature, soon made my peaceful, cosy life a living nightmare. There was nothing else for it. It had to die.

This wasn't something I could rush into, I had to bide my time. The adults doted on it 24/7, I couldn't get even close. There wasn't much of a window to attack without getting busted, and I didn't want to arouse suspicion; doing so could potentially thwart my plans and possibly make me prime suspect after the deed was done. I had to think ahead and that required patience, patience I didn't have.

In addition to the perpetual noise the new arrival smelt really, really bad. The grown ups seemed to be permanently shoving food in one end only for it to arrive out of the other.

To make matter even worse I was getting even less attention. To pass the time of day I found that scribbling on walls and excreting in unusual places soon got me noticed, but unless I was kicking up a stink I was flatly ignored. On one occasion it took one of the grown ups three days to realise that the muddy looking stuff I was pushing around in the back of my Corgi flat bed Land Rover wasn't actually mud.

Soon the creature was crawling around on its belly, I seemed to be the main source of its interest which meant it would suddenly appear, uninvited, and fuck with my stuff. This was the last straw, at least when it was unable to move it wasn't ingratiating itself into my world of action men and drawing implements. Now it was permanently appearing in my space, destroying fleets of carefully arranged vehicles and tearing apart Lego based housing projects. The second I rightfully rejected its attention with a casual slap to the face, a grown up would appear, stand over me and read the riot act prior to a bout of solitary confinement in my bedroom. What had I done? Soon, I thought, my time will come...

Then came the day that it was upright, wobbling on its two fat little legs. It didn't take it long to discover that, whilst unstable, it could speedily escape from the grown ups. Isolated from its protectors it was at my mercy, still being its main source of attention, it was me it came to. The fool. Come into my parlour said the spider to the fly as it "fell" down the stairs, twice. It also "walked" into the pond and "choked" on a Sticklebrick. In one last hopeless effort I lured it to the garden shed and sprayed it with greenfly killer, it danced in the mist of death before a grown up found us, separated me from my breath and the creature was rushed to hospital, so very close but so very far.

By now I was beginning to run out of heinous ideas and my willpower was flagging. I watched it eating glass baubles off the Christmas tree, and it conveniently "found" tools with which to desecrate the wallpaper and skirting boards. Obviously the grown ups needed to be informed of this wilful, vicious act of wanton vandalism.

Sadly it was all in vain, the creature seemed to bounce, always re-appearing unscathed and despite bouts of slapping, biting and the odd punch it kept returning for more of the same. It seemed to actually *like* being punished; slowly my murderous intent was ground down by its tenacity; such tolerance for pain! Such a desire to live!

The worm was beginning to turn, I became fearful of it, I couldn't understand why on earth it wanted to stay. What was slightly more problematic was that it seemed to be one step ahead of me all the time, it was already in my bedroom when I woke up, and even in the middle of the night it would suddenly appear and attempt to climb into my bed. As time went on I grew used to its presence and my campaign of violence was spurned in favour of random half hearted assaults. I also dis-

covered that I wasn't too happy if someone else attacked the creature, she was mine to attack; those that attacked were themselves, attacked. Yeah, I suppose I could live with it, so long as it let me eat its sweets when I felt like it...

Then one awful autumn day another one appeared, out of the blue. Not again I thought, not again! I turned to face my sister; she was staring at it with barely concealed hatred, her little mouth turned down in a visage of horror and confusion. Now at last she knew how it felt, now at last I had partner. I looked at my sister and I looked at this new tiny little creature. For him it was going to be a long, cold winter. ◉

SWYN

CRAP NIGHTS OUT

ANNUAL CEMENT CONVENTION

Katie Maskell digs herself into a hole

Looking back, the clues were in the titles. The Fox and Hounds Hotel Ladies Darts B Team's Bi-Annual Outing. Kerry-Ann Lee's Second Hen Weekend on a barge in Manchester (in November). And the PR Girls of Callella's Sexy Summer Knees Up at a Mexican Themed Irish Bar run by two Peruvians on the Costa Brava. "Mambo Number Five" was played on a loop. I tried clicking my heels together three times saying "There's no place like a physics re-sit," but "a little bit of Monica" played on.

None of these crap nights out were quite as crap as the CF (Cement Federation) Christmas Dinner and Dance in Grantham 2004 where I was the Cordially Invited Guest, in my capacity of girlfriend of R_ Cement. I was not girlfriend to R_ Cement itself, but the girlfriend of a "Friend of R_ Cement" ("Friend" meaning any other independent builder's merchant in the North).

We drove the two hours or so to Grantham with Steve, my boyfriend's boss, and his girlfriend Helen. Along the way Helen drew my attention to various landmarks and points of interest. Or at least she would have done had there been any but, as the drive from Wakefield to Grantham is remarkable only for the unusual quantity of signs for Craft Fairs, she pointed them out instead. Steve and my boyfriend talked about cement.

The dress code was Black Tie/Glamorous. I had tried to think "glamour" when I went shopping for a frock, but the word "cement" kept intruding and I ended up thinking "glament" or "cementerous" or something and bought a little grey number that gaped at the chest. It was intended to gape I think, but it needed some cleavage to put where my sternum sat. "Anyway," I thought, "Less is probably more". Which, on arriving and seeing the other frocks, I saw was wrong. More was more. Less was less. Spades were spades. I had lived in London too long and had started thinking a spade might be any number of things, and that glamorous might mean grey and flat chested.

When my boyfriend introduced me to June, I saw what kind of glamour it was the cement world wanted. Top shelf stuff. June, who seemed to be girlfriend to the whole of R_ Cement (and all of its "friends" as well) held the proud honour of being the only female in the room who had been invited in her own right, and not as anyone's wife/latest bit of fluff. She nearly had my boyfriend's eye out on her nipples. I stuck out my sternum. The older ladies were squeezed into second skin sequins and had feathers in their up-dos. Geriatric Mardi Gras with corned beef coloured legs.

We were entertained through dinner by Basil and Sybil Fawlty lookie/soundie-likies. I stared at June's nipples and drank a bottle of wine and two Irish coffees to see me through the speeches. Opposite was Karen. During the award giving for highest sales of sand in Stockport, she leaned in and shouted over, "I'm more of a people person myself. There's only so much you can say about sand. What do you do?"

It was hard to communicate over the applause. "I work in an office," I said. "I'm an assistant..."

"A what?"

I said, "they look after writers."

"You what?"

I shout "SCRIPTS."

She raises an eyebrow. "Oh," she says, "Well. Nothing to be ashamed of. Looking never hurt anyone."

"SCRIPTS!" I shout, "NOT STRIP!"

"If you've got it..."

The speeches were over. Karen went to the toilet. Flattered that she thought I could be a stripper, I took my boyfriend to the bar where I was introduced to the MD of R_ Cement. He was 5'4" and looked like Lovejoy. He wanted to dance. I didn't. My boyfriend, casting around for June's nipples, said "Go on." and buggered off. He ground his way through the *Grease* Medley, groped through "Dirty Dancing" and when "When A Man Loves A Woman" came on I grabbed a passing "Sybil," and asked her to point me to the

THE GLAMOROUS WORLD OF CEMENT

toilet. Mr. Cement handed me his business card and said "Your boyfriend doesn't deserve you". I agreed but was a good few drinks from thinking an aged midget Lovejoy lookie likie might make a happy alternative.

On my way to the toilet, I passed Karen. She gave me a filthy look. Her friend said loudly "Well, she doesn't look like much of a stripper". I was insulted. I looked at myself in the mirror. It was true. My makeup had run. I looked like cement. I went in search of my boyfriend to ask if we could leave. We couldn't.

Standing by my man, while June sat in his lap, I drank someone else's brandy, and pondered the meaning of love and decided it wasn't my boyfriend, or Lovejoy. I heard Elton sing "It seems to me you lived your life like a candle in the wind" and I wasn't sure if it was the one about Marilyn Monroe or the one about Princess Diana but I thought "how true", of both of them, and also "how true of me" and then I dropped my fag down my sternum. I couldn't disentangle my boyfriend from June so I clicked my heels together three times and said "There's no place like a Mexican Themed Irish Bar run by two Peruvians on the Costa Brava" but "Candle in the Wind" played on. 🐚

PETE LOVEDAY

NEW RANGE OF IDLER
T-SHIRTS IS AVAIABLE

idler Logo

Work Kills

Big snail

Snail Rainbow

Lady of Leisure

Spiral Snails

Spiral Snails

Big snail

Snail Rainbow

AT WWW.IDLER.CO.UK

IT'S A LAZY, LAZY, LAZY WORLD

A glossary of global idling terms by Adam Jacot de Boinod

KOPUHIA (Rapa Nui, Easter Island) someone who disappears instead of dedicating himself to his work

LINTI (Persian) someone who idles away his day lying under a tree

BETTSCHWERE (German) without the energy to get out of bed

NUBIE YAM (Waali, Ghana) a farmer who points to his farm, but does little more (literally, finger farm)

GOBER LES MOUCHES (French) to stand by idly (literally, to gulp down flies)

ZAMZAMA (Arabic) to waft along in a relaxed style

GOYANG KAKI (Indonesia) relaxing and enjoying oneself as problems are sorted out by others (literally, to swing one's legs)

KALINCAK-KELINCOK (Balinese, Indonesia) the back and forth, here and there or up and down of genuine drifting

LUFTMENSCH (Yiddish) an impractical dreamer having no definite business or income

VIAJOU NA MAIONESE (Portugese) to live in a dream world (literally, to travel in the mayonnaise)

NGLAYAP (Indonesian) to wander far from from home with no particular purpose

UMUDROVAT SE (Czech) to philosophize oneself into the madhouse

FUCHA (Polish) to use company time and resources for one's own purposes

HAOCHI-LANZUO (Chinese) to be fond of food and averse to work

AVIADOR (Spanish, Central America) a government employee who shows up only on payday

CHUPOTERO (Spanish) a person who works little but has several salaries

MADOGIWAZOKU (Japanese) those who have little to do (literally, window gazers)

MÉTRO-BOULOT-DODO (French), tube-work-sleep, expressing the pointless grind of life

Extracted from The Meaning of Tingo
by Adam Jacot de Boinod, Penguin, £10.00.
Copyright © Adam Jacot de Boinod. Illustrations
© Sandra Howgate. www.penguin.co.uk

By Tony Husband

BILL AND ZED'S BAD ADVICE

WE'VE FUCKED UP OUR LIVES. NOW IT'S YOUR TURN

DEAR BILL AND ZED,

My question concerns socialising with work colleagues. Recently, I was press-ganged into after work drinks that ended in a karaoke bar, where—to my lasting shame—I found myself performing MC Hammer's "U Can't Touch This". Needless to say, no one wanted to touch it, no matter how many times I forbade them.

Then I refused to join in the vodka drinking games, pointing out that such irresponsibility encourages people to imbibe far more than is helpful or wise. One of my colleagues confronted me and demanded to know exactly when I had become "such a sanctimonious, self-righteous prick"? It seemed that it was not enough that I gamely humiliate myself by attempting to rap, I must also make myself sick with booze.

Must I be a mong to get on?
Adrift, Sheffield

ZED: Socialising with work colleagues? Tell me about it, dear boy. Imagine what it is like to have a work colleague like mine.

Every time the old chanteuse Billy boy gets himself bladdered, he frog marches me down to Madame JoJos , where I have to sit for hour after hour watching as Corby's worst female drag queen, madame Billy herself, mimes along hysterically to Shirley Basset, Cher and all the rest.

As for the drinking games, I sympathize entirely, I mean, how many innocent homosexuals do you have to beat to

within an inch of their lives before that boring old drinking game "Gaybashing" becomes a total drag.

The only drinking game I really enjoy is Russian Roulette, if only for the fact that one day Madame Billy might win and blow his fucking brains out.

Try and get your work friends to play this traditional Slavic drinking game and provided you're lucky your work friends should start declining rapidly in their irritating numbers.

Good luck!

BILL: Well, Zed can fuck off for a start. It was him that wanted to go to Madame JoJos in the first place. It was him that got booed off doing "Je Ne Regrette Rien". And it was me that got cheered and cheered for my rendition of "Gypsies, Tramps and Thieves". Anyway, right now I've got far more important things to be doing than sorting out you lot's problems. So you will have no choice but to forgive me for the brevity of my advice, bad or good, in this issue of the Idler. As for Mr Adrift, Zed is correct. Get yourself a revolver and one bullet. After a game of Russian roulette sex will be the best you've ever had.

.....

DEAR BILL AND ZED,

I was out with my family when a mentally ill man was drawn inexorably toward me. His name was Alfie, which he thought made some people jealous. Perhaps that was why they locked him away. For six

CHRIS WATSON

years. "Do you see what I mean?" he asked again and again, hopelessly suggesting common ground. "Man-to-man, Already I know they are going to come and get me and put me away forever. One thing. I do one thing wrong, and I am away forever."

We walked together for some way until he asked me to pray for him. And I did. But I could have done a great deal more.
All Mixed Up, Liverpool

ZED: Well Mr Mix, sir, yes, you could have done a lot more, The poor fellow probably hadn't had sex since he got out of jail. What would have been wrong with giving the poor fellow a little man-to-man tramp buggery relief. I'm sure that's what he really wanted and that is exactly what my generous, altruistic, saintly friend Bill would have done.

BILL: They haven't let fucking Alfie out? He was a friend of mine back when punk rock was... anyway this Alfie shot and killed his sister. Then chopped off his mum's right hand with a meat cleaver just because I tried to shag the pair of them. I knew if they ever let Alfie out he would start it all up again. Go and find him and do the decent thing for society: stab him seven times in the heart. As for the buggery, forget it, they never appreciate it.

.....

DEAR BILL AND ZED,

I asked a woman for her bloke's mobile phone number, as I needed him to do some work for me. Unfortunately, she became wild and jealous and accused me of wanting to steal him from her. She insisted on coming over to my workplace and calling me a whore in front of everyone. I was wondering if you have any insight into staying out of trouble in the continent.
Miss Exile, Tanzania

ZED: Dear Tanzanian exile, I don't believe a fucking word of your innocent protestations, you dirty slag.

Asked him over to do some work for you, yeah, yeah, yeah and we all know what kind of work that would be don't we? His wife was right to call you a whore in front of your friends, because you are!

How do I know this?
Simple.
All women are liars and whores.
How do I justify this outrageous assumption?

Again, simple. I justify my opinions with exactly the same logic and authority that, that fat dungaree wearing lesbo from the seventies did when she decreed that all men are rapists.

Sheer demented sexual predjudice.

BILL: Andrea Dworkin is one of the most beautiful women I have never met. I didn't think this before I started reading her work. Once I read it, my eyes were opened. She stands head and shoulders above all her American feminist sisters. As for African customs, it is impossible to stay out of trouble in Africa. Africa was made for trouble. That is why it exists. As for you being a whore, I think that must just be your fantasy. ◉

CONVERSATIONS

In conversation with

Michael Palin

TOM HODGKINSON **MEETS THE AMIABLE COMEDY GENIUS TURNED GLOBAL TRAVELLER. CONTEMPORARY PHOTOGRAPHS BY** RACHEL POULTON

WE APPROACHED Michael Palin after we'd seen him being interviewed on telly saying that he'd lived in the same small house since 1968. Despite his fame and fortune, he'd never bothered to move. He had also just performed a one-man show in the West End called *Forty Years Without a Proper Job*. So it seemed he might have some wisdom to impart for those of us pursuing the idle life. We met Palin in his office near Covent Garden.

IDLER: How often do you come into the office?
PALIN: It varies, sometimes twice a week. I like the location here. Covent Garden is up there… Holborn and east London is not so far away and you can walk down to Waterloo Bridge.
IDLER: So you've just had your show, *Forty Years Without A Proper Job*, and you've said recently on a TV interview that your life has happened rather than being planned, that you had no burning ambition. It seems that this idea has been on your mind.
PALIN: The title of the show came from a practical consideration. This show was going to be just about my life, so I thought, are there any themes to it all? The fact is I've never really had a job. I've

never signed a contract longer than six to eight weeks. So I thought, well, that gets me out of appearing to be an expert on anything, or having to declare a direction to my life. It really is pretty close to how my life has been. Very fortunately I've managed to avoid the issue of getting a proper job or deciding what I am best at or I'm good at. It goes back to my father—he had been brought up in two world wars and through the recession of the 1930s. It was a rough time, so after that the children were jolly well going to be comfortable and secure and follow a certain pattern, and part of that was having a proper job. I remember worrying throughout my education, as my particular talents lay not in any practical direction: I was not good at maths or mechanics or chemistry. The only thing I really wanted to do was to be an airline pilot for a bit, but then I realised that for that you needed maths... all the other things were to do with internal ambition and imagination. I've always had a rather busy, productive imagination and that led more to things that you couldn't quantify as being useful such as writing and acting. Those were the areas where whatever talent I had lay, so it was hard to reconcile this with my father's desire for me to get a proper job. But then I learned that my father, who was an engineer, had never wanted to be an engineer. He had wanted to be a church chorister, or church organist. He loved church music. He really wanted to be at Cambridge or somewhere like that and sing in the choir and his father said "no, you've got a get a proper job."

IDLER: And he passed that down to you, he hadn't looked back and thought that was a mistake?

PALIN: Well, we didn't really talk about things like that. He didn't say, "here's an irony, lad! There I am, trying to get you a proper job, and all I would have liked to been was this." He steadily maintained that he was a working man, he went to work, he came back in the evening at the same time and all that... so yes, I thought it would be a good title.

IDLER: It seems that musicians and pop stars, often, are actually motivated by the fact

TOM AND MICHAEL SHOOT THE BREEZE

that they don't want to get out of bed before lunchtime. That comes first. You sit in your bedsit all day on the dole and that gets you out onto a different path. Were you actually consciously motivated to do things that weren't jobs?

PALIN: I was always insatiably curious about people and life, and I read a lot. The motivation was really just to try and reconcile the need to work with some particular talent and inclination. I had a fairly secure upbringing. Although my father didn't have much money, he did send me to a private preparatory school, and then I went away to Shrewsbury School. They provided a sort of structure. I thought that during that period something would come along, like puberty, but in terms of work, a desire to be an executive or work in a bank. You would wake up one morning and think, yes, this is what I have to do. But it never happened. I always enjoyed acting, which is a dangerously subversive talent in a way. You look at schoolmasters who are doing a perfectly good job and you become fascinated by the way they touch their left ear when they talk, or the way their trousers are very, very, very wrinkled around the crotch and things like that. These were the thoughts that came into my mind... I knew there

"I'VE ALWAYS HAD A BUSY, PRODUCTIVE IMAGINATION THAT LED MORE TO THINGS THAT YOU COULDN'T QUANTIFY AS BEING USEFUL"

FOSSALTA DI PIAVE, ITALY

was a financial imperative. My father had given up half his income to send me to school. So there was no question that he would support me. And just by a series of really lucky encounters I ended up doing two things: one was working with Terry Jones, who I'd met at Oxford. He'd left a year before me, and was writing a thing called *The Love Show*, a theatrical documentary about sex through the ages. He said, would I help him write it. It was an interesting project but paid very little. Then, quite out of the blue, a friend's girlfriend knew a journalist who was writing a new comedy pop show called *Now!* on TWW in Wales. Would I like to audition as a presenter? Without telling my father, I went up and I got this job. It was 1965 and it just involved introducing a lot of pop groups and doing rather bad jokes.

IDLER: So that was a fantastic time for music.

PALIN: Yes, we used to get groups there like John Mayall, Eric Clapton, the Small Faces, Georgie Fame, Alan Price...

IDLER: I saw *O' Lucky Man* the other day... a great film...

PALIN: Yes, a mess, but a mess you have to see. At that time it did seem that you were liberated from whatever had gone before. I was a provincial boy, born and brought up in Sheffield, so to come to London just at the time of The Beatles and Twiggy and Mary Quant... it was the place to be. There was a feeling that there were opportunities to do something new and fresh. Although, the old hierarchies were still there. The BBC, which I ended up working for, on *The Frost Report* and eventually *Monty Python*, was run in quite a conventional way, by mainly men. It harped back to

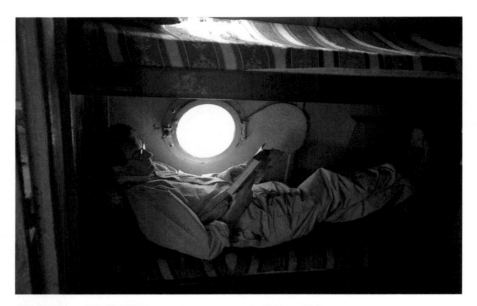

BASIL PAO

TOP: THE SAHARA BY TRAIN
BOTTOM: NATIVE AMERICAN SLOT MACHINE IN PETSOKEY MICHIGAN

an ideal age of the Reithian twenties or thirties. Things were changing on one level but not on another. What was really happening was that young people coming out of university and art school especially, felt that they could do anything. But at the same time, people at the top level were saying, "not so fast, we're still in control." So there was a conflict there that made things work better, for us.

IDLER: If you imagine yourself at that age now, do you think things are less exciting? Are prospects better or worse for idlers today?

PALIN: Aaaah… It's terribly hard as I don't really know what's in the mind of a young person… but I think that in a sense, when we did *Monty Python* there were far more restrictions against that form of expression, that sort of free-form comedy. You could be inventive but you'd go out late at night; if you got too popular you'd get censored for saying "bum" or "shit"… now there's a feeling that everything is permitted, apart from racial jokes. You can say what you want and that's left people a bit bewildered. There was such an establishment when we were writing *Python* in the late sixties, and the Army and the Church and a very male-dominated traditional society was still in place. So we could have lots of jokes at their expense. We had censorship, the Lord Chamberlain had instructions on nudity on television. We were naughty, cheeky, mischievous little boys able to carry our naughty, mischievous ways into early middle age. I think the fact that *Python* is still popular among kids of ten, eleven, twelve is because they see something in it which is still outside the general run of comedy. Why that is I'm not quite sure, except that *Python* was a mish-mash: bits of film, animation, satire, pure silliness. The films were really well made, great credit to Terry Gilliam for making them look so good. With *Life of Brian*, we always knew we'd have some problems because of the subject matter. The most serious act of censorship was when the head of EMI, who had financed the film–and we already had people in Tunisia building sets–suddenly read the script. He said "Who's tricked me into this? We can't do this, absolutely not." He refused to touch it. And that's when George Harrison came in. It was something like five million pounds, and someone said to George, "why did you do it?" and George said, "well, I just wanted to see it." A very good reason, and of course, being a Beatle, he had a lot of money.

IDLER: I've been reading Abbie Hoffman and Jerry Rubin's books, the sixties underground heroes, and they always cite the Beatles as an influence. They pulled off this trick of being massive and also underground at the same time. And I suppose Python was quite similar… the hippies also liked the Beatles' non-hierarchical way of working, as a family rather than climbing up a ladder.

PALIN: We both had a certain wariness of the world outside trying to market us or pull us in a certain direction, and for both The Beatles and *Python*, the work was the important thing. If you were successful that was great, but it was about the work. You didn't bring in consultants to tell you what you should do, you didn't do audience research, as people do now. There were no showings for potential audiences saying what they liked. You did your own thing. The peer group was the little group you were working with. No one ever got in the way of that, all the decisions were taken by the group. So I think the reason why pop groups liked *Python* and why Abbie Hoffman liked the Beatles was that we seemed to embody an artistic freedom, a creative freedom. A creative freedom that was also successful… you could see the

"HA HA, THE IDEA IS TO GET PAID FOR SOMETHING YOU REALLY WANT TO DO!"

Beatles going round the world being screamed at. It was like a very benign revolution. There were people of sixteen, seventeen, eighteen who should have been at school going to airports shouting, "we love you, yeah yeah yeah!" And The Beatles weren't manipulative. The sense people got of them being free spirits was true. And I suppose there was a certain amount of that in *Python* as well.

IDLER: There were no precedents... I suppose today that all comedy groups are going to have *Monty Python* at the back of their heads as a model, and every band certainly thinks about The Beatles.

PALIN: There was no precedent, but we drew inspiration from certain areas. Spike Milligan's *Q* series was influential on the shape the *Python* shows took. Although *Python* was off the wall and unstructured there was actually quite a lot of debate in the early days about the form it should take. In the end we came up with the idea of the stream of consciousness, which got us out of all sorts of problems.. we had sketches that didn't end, suddenly cutting to film... but that was inspired by Spike's series, he just did silly things. At the BBC at the time someone once had appeared in a costume drama without removing the label saying who they were, and that was one of the great crimes. Spike's way of dealing with that was to have labels on everyone, the name of the actor plus their take-home pay... that freewheeling approach we liked. But there was no other group quite like it... *Do Not Adjust Your Set* and *At Last, the 1948 Show* were sort of like that... university-influenced people that would previously have been on smokers' revues... but they were conventional in their form. *Python* didn't have a precedent. I think that the way the six of us interacted, was something you couldn't have ever worked out, for all the computer modeling, research or auditions. We weren't the Spice Girls. When we came together the humour just crackled, and on a good day it worked so well that that you felt that these were the only people in the world you wanted to be with. We were very different.

Having Gilliam, the American input, the animations, that was important. Graham Chapman was an odd character, rather distant, smoked his pipe, but came out with the most brilliant off-the-wall ideas. Having John Cleese, who looked the perfect establishment character, who absolutely represents authority, be completely zany and silly and able to send himself up… it was all there. But what we felt at the time, was that we would have two or three good years and then someone else would come along and we would do something else. People weren't expected to last that long.

IDLER: One of the problems I think now is that your chosen pursuit, comedy or writing or whatever it might be, is seen right from the beginning as a career path. Then it just becomes a job going up a ladder. Things should be deprofessionalised, we should bring out the amateur.

PALIN: I absolutely agree with that. Underneath you're looking for some kind of security. I was very lucky in that early on I made money from comedy, which was the last thing I expected to happen. I knew I could write, so advertising or journalism were possibilities. Through *Do Not Adjust Your Set* I had enough money to get married and get a flat in London. People want to be as free as possible, but you need a certain basis of comfort and security and I did get that fairly early on.

IDLER: When it comes to money, have you done things that later you wish you hadn't done because you did them for the money? Or has the money, though welcome, always been the second priority?

PALIN: Ha ha, the idea is to get paid for something you really want to do! Yes, there were things early on. I did quite a lot of radio commercials just because they paid well and we needed the money. At that time there was no career path. As soon as John wanted to wind *Python* down we realised that there was no more *Python*. It was only after a couple of years of doing other things that we got the film together and it revived. So right into the early seventies, we were doing commercials, which I wasn't particularly proud of, largely because I had a glimpse into that world. Being asked to advertise something which you don't have any strong feelings about, a dog food or an instant coffee… you were restricted in what you could say: you were generally working to a script that someone else had worked out. Everything seemed wrong about it. Instead of your peer group of five others you would have ten people squeezed into a gallery, saying, "can you do it a bit more Welsh, can you do it in a slightly higher tone, not Welsh but Welsh borders…" You had people putting their oar in for no particular reason other than they were in the advertising business and they wanted to show that at the end of the day that they'd done some work. That's a terrible problem. And I realised I didn't like doing these, I was a performing dog. But on the other hand we needed the money and I was grateful to be asked. But they were some of the worst things I ever remember doing. Apart from that I've been fortunate in that from early on, I've had a considerable say in what I've done, as a writer and performer.

IDLER: You say it's luck, but the existential idea is that doing and choosing are the same thing. So is it pure luck or are you guiding yourself into certain positions?

BASIL PAO

THE TERRACE OF THE GRITTI PALACE HOTEL, VENICE

PALIN: Whatever talent I had lay in acting and in writing. I noticed the comedy in life and the absurdity. Humour was the main reaction to things I saw around me. That was good because the sort of people you met had similar thoughts and tastes, and they were slightly subversive, they weren't the ones who said that life is terribly serious. I was worried about it at one time, someone at school said "have you seriously thought about your life?" It turned out he'd become a Born Again Christian and I thought, there goes a good friend, but maybe I should be more serious... maybe this flippancy is something I should grow out of. But it carried on and I made certain friends, people like a man called Robert Hewison, who I met at university. He was from London, very bright, really metropolitan, he was hip and I was a hick. But we got together because we had a similar sense of humour, we liked Spike Milligan and all that. I chose him as my friend and vice versa. Out of all the people I knew at Oxford he made the vital decision of saying, "let's not just tell each other jokes, let's get together a half hour cabaret act and we can make money from this." And I thought, "make money from laughing?" And I realised that not being serious could be a way of making a living. And by the time that I'd done a review at the Edinburgh Festival, and David Frost had come up and talent-scouted us, I realised even more.. all I'm saying really is that the various connections I've made in my life and the people I've met have been very, very important. Robert pushed me into performing which I would probably never have done because I was sort of shy, Terry Jones led me into writing after I'd left university. I've fallen into things because I've been there at the right time with the right people. I wouldn't say I'm a great one at taking the initiative. With the travel programmes, it wasn't me saying, "I want to do travel programmes". It's just that when someone came to me with the idea of *Around the World in Eighty Days*, I realised that I loved travelling, and that this was a lovely way of not making a decision of what I really should do in life. And here I am, I'm sixty-two and I still have no real idea of what I ought to be doing! But travelling and *Python* gave me some sort of purpose.

IDLER: So you found your gift, but it's been the processes and living itself rather than the achievements and goals that have characterized your life?

PALIN: Yes, I still regard it as something wonderful, to be alive now, to be in London, whatever... I'm wary of people who appear to have changed, who say, "I'm not the person I was at eighteen." I'm the person I was at eighteen, I'm the person I was at seven. I can feel that connection, and that combination of apprehension about what lay ahead but intense curiosity about what lay ahead. I like to hope that my reactions now are still as fresh as they always used to be.

IDLER: You said recently that you have contemporaries who have made a lot of money and gone on to buy second houses in the country and burdened themselves with all these problems, but that you've decided to stay in the same house you've always lived in.

PALIN: Well, I realised when I heard that on the interview that there I was talking about people who have other houses and my wife said, "what are you saying? We've got three houses." I still live in the same house that we bought in 1968. And we've bought the house on either side. They're actually quite small houses, so we have expanded... and they're in the same street and there are only four houses in the street, so I've got to be very, very careful! They are individual houses, one is separate from the other and the other one is knocked through.

IDLER: A bit like the Beatles in *Help!*

PALIN: A bit like that, so I've got to be careful about pointing the finger.

IDLER: I suppose it's idlerish, in that you bought the next door house, rather than...

"I'M WARY OF PEOPLE WHO APPEAR TO HAVE CHANGED, WHO SAY, 'I'M NOT THE PERSON I WAS AT EIGHTEEN.'"

PALIN: Yes, there's been no quantum leap into massive country houses, but I've toyed with that. And at one time, I thought this is what you do when you've got a bit of money, you buy a second home somewhere out of London.

IDLER: I remember David Gilmour said he suddenly realized "what's the point in having all these houses, it's just a pain in the arse and you can only live in one."

PALIN: My wife's been very, very important in this. We've been together now for forty years, so what she thinks influences me and vice versa, and we're both reasonably placid, we're not driven by a great ambition to own lots of things. I did go through a phase where I thought, "I've got to get somewhere bigger, I've got to get a house in Hampstead."

IDLER: Because you thought you ought to?

PALIN: Because I could, I suppose. At that time, if you could buy a house with a moat somewhere in Oxfordshire, you did. But we realised that where we were, Gospel Oak in London NW5, was very convenient, we were on the edge of Hampstead Heath, we could park our car right outside our house. As Hunter Davies said, "he is pleasantly wedded to the unfashionable side of the Heath." But it's great. I now realize that you can waste an awful lot of time buying things, and I never had that time. I was always doing things, projects that interested me. Being a provincial, and never having felt part of London, I now really value being in the city. I like art, I like the movies. You forget how lucky you are to have cinemas that show films from eastern Europe. I read the the other day that only 14% of people between 55 and 64 go to the cinema more than once a year. I couldn't believe it. But outside London there's no cinemas, you just don't have them. You have the multiplexes, you're probably better off buying the DVD. Where I am I've got the Renoir, the Everyman, the Screen... I'm just raving on about London... but I don't want a lot of clutter now. What's the point?

IDLER: And the thing that you related that to in the interview, was that instead of spending any free time you've got buying things, you either want to be working or staring out of the window... is that true?

PALIN: I enjoy working, but there is a mixture of cowardice and laziness in the choices I make. I would love to write another novel, I wrote one novel, *Hemingway's Chair* in 1994, and I haven't really had the courage to write a second one. I'd like to, but I know that means at least six months of saying "no" to everything else, and trying to work out something in your head. My imagination is quite fertile, but I've avoided that issue. It's the same thing with acting on stage. I love appearing on stage, I'm reasonably shy but I have a degree of exhibitionism.

IDLER: Do you feel nervous before you go on stage?

PALIN: Yes. In my experience, if you don't feel nervous, then you've really had it: the concentration goes. It's not a natural thing, to walk out in front of an audience, whether it's twenty people or two thousand people. Each time it's a leap in the dark. I've never felt, "this is my role in life, I'm rather good at it and people should accept that." I wish I could feel that comfortable confidence. I don't: every time I feel, "here we go again." Like the thing the other night. There were a thousand people there, and

TOP: MID SIXTIES, HAMPSTEAD PUB. BOTTOM: TWW. MANFRED MANN, PETER COOK, HELEN PALIN, MICHAEL, PAUL JONES AND DUDLEY MOORE

FISH SLAPPING DANCE, TEDDINGTON LOCK, 1971

although I knew I'd probably be OK, and I had material I'd done before, it just doesn't feel like that when you're about to go on. But that's good. It's what I mean about still being uncertain about what life really is and what one's role in life is. I just don't see it all tied up yet. *Around The World in Eighty Days*, was great, it came out of the blue, but I wasn't the only one who was asked. Other people with slightly more structured lives like Alan Whicker and Miles Kington said "no". They're probably kicking themselves now. I was happy to take the risk. It struck a chord with me; it wasn't someone forcing me and it wasn't someone telling me that I'd make more money doing this, although it has turned out to be quite lucrative. I try not to make a huge difference between work and non-work. It's rather like the fallacy of holidays. You go on holiday and think you'll be happy, totally happy, and come back, and God, you're back into work. But you've got to realize that holidays are very hard work and as stressful as any business meeting. But if you can build into your work a little bit of time to do things that you enjoy... so that's the great thing about having this office. If I've got a half hour I can go to the Courtauld Gallery, or I can go over the bridge, or the Portrait Gallery, or on the way here I can just stop and have a coffee and sit... Café life I absolutely love, I can do a bit of the old flâneuring knowing that I'm coming to work. You can build in time just to ruminate, and amble, which I think is quite important, at the same time as working rather hard. Because if I didn't do the work, then I think I might just sit at home, and I would do a lot of displacement activity and I wouldn't be any freer, I wouldn't have any more time than I have when I'm working. I wouldn't be using my mind and brain and seeing things.

IDLER: A conclusion I've come to at the *Idler* is that it starts with retreating from work but it's really about making work into something that isn't drudgery and slavery, and then work and life can become one thing.

PALIN: You can have work which expands your horizons, which can enrich your view of the

"I TRY NOT TO MAKE A HUGE DIFFERENCE BETWEEN WORK AND NON-WORK. IT'S RATHER LIKE THE FALLACY OF HOLIDAYS..."

MONTY PYTHON AT THE HOLLYWOOD BOWL, 1980 L TO R, MICHAEL PALIN, TERRY JONES, ERIC IDLE, GRAHAM CHAPMAN, TERRY GILLIAM AND JOHN CLEESE

world, or you can have work which controls and restricts and which you can't wait to get away from. I'm lucky, because I've been freelance, and I've avoided doing things that I'm not very good at. I am aware sometimes that when I have to go to meetings I don't want to go to, or I get marketing guff thrown at me, what an awful fate awaits you if you get on the treadmill. Which a lot of people just have to do. Although you don't absolutely have to…

IDLER: Yes, do we have to? Maybe people are actually freer than they think; we somehow choose to enslave ourselves. I've done it. It's quite difficult to see what the alternatives are. Unless you're confident and courageous to start with, it's hard to do your own thing.

PALIN: Although I wonder if it's easier nowadays. My generation had to get a proper job, and a job for life. So if you could sign up with a company, or one of the professions, then that was the one thing you ought to do. Because of what had gone before, the mass unemployment and so on. But now, it doesn't seem the same. I don't know, maybe this is just a London view or maybe I'm looking at my own children who are all doing things they enjoy doing, but now you don't have to sign up for life. In fact a lot of companies don't want you for life. So in a way, that might help. You may not like the job, but it's going to come to an end in six weeks. Certainly my children have built networks of people who do feel that you can change within the work that you're doing. From what I've seen, it's a better time for people who seek self-realization, and find what they can do best, and get paid for it, than perhaps it was in the sixties. It's a more creative time, in music and fashion and design and architecture. Things are much better now. Everyone has loosened up a bit... the other side of it is that we don't respect, in the same way, the institutions.

IDLER: But some of them have become so enormous, like Tesco's, that they're threatening to take over the country.

PALIN: I was thinking more of the Church and the Army, and the way they dominated. But I suppose there are other things. But I'm generally an optimist. Although you do have supermarkets everywhere and all that, you also have, certainly where we live, little shops opening that weren't there before. Our corner shops are much better now. People go out to restaurants a lot more: my parents would go out once every six months. That's a good thing because people meet each other. We have lots of Polish delicatessants opening because there are lot of Poles in London but also because people don't want to go into the West End... I think that it's a pretty good time to be alive now.

IDLER: The immigrants are bringing a lot of life and fun and interest and variety and also independent places.

PALIN: I like all that. What I just hate is conformity. Whether it was something trivial like having to wear a DJ, one of my pet hates, at formal dinner events so everyone can look the same, or something much bigger like the feeling that you can't say what you want to say. But it comes back in different ways. Political correctness is very strong. We could say, "miserable fat Belgian bastard", before but now people would feel rather uncomfortable about that. Well, it's very interesting to talk and to ramble. Actually, I'm going off to see Robert Hewison now, funnily enough. We still keep up. ◉

"WHAT I HATE IS CONFORMITY... LIKE THE FEELING THAT YOU CAN'T SAY WHAT YOU WANT TO SAY"

FEATURES

Learning to Live

MATTHEW APPLETON **DESCRIBES THE HISTORY AND THE PRESENT OF A.S. NEILL'S FREEDOM-SEEKING SUMMERHILL SCHOOL. PHOTOGRAPHS BY** MATTHEW APPLETON

> "Many pupils have been allowed to mistake the pursuit of idleness
> for the exercise of personal liberty."
> Ofsted Report.

THE "DO-AS-YOU-LIKE" SCHOOL

A few days ago I dropped off my 13-year-old daughter, Eva, at Summerhill School for the new term. I was in her room helping her unpack, when a couple of girls rushed in to announce that a particularly annoying boy was on his way. Eva quickly locked the door and got on with unpacking. Moments later there was knocking, and a boy's voice calling her name. She rolled her eyes and ignored it. After a few seconds of banging loudly he shouted "Bitch!" and threatened to find an axe to smash the door down with, before stomping off. Eva, completely unperturbed, continued her unpacking. Later as we left the room a spray of water hit me straight in the face and I found myself looking at three girls, who were dissolving into a mixture of giggles and apologies. They had been waiting to ambush Eva or one of the other girls in the room, and did not expect a parent to emerge. Eva found it just as funny as they did.

The atmosphere was more like that of a large family than a school: a family in which adults were included as equals. Some adults might find it uncomfortable to be treated as one of the crowd, rather than a figure of authority. Some parents might find it disconcerting to find strange boys calling their daughter a bitch and threatening to

NEIL BELIEVED THAT CHILDREN ARE ESSENTIALLY GOOD BY NATURE

destroy her bedroom door with an axe. But I felt very at home at Summerhill as, indeed, it had been my home for nine years, when I had lived and worked at the school as a houseparent. Eight years have passed since then, but the easy-going flow of interactions between kids of all ages and adults was familiar terrain to me. It did not occur to me for a moment that the boy at the door was going to turn into a pre-adolescent version of Jack Nicholson in *The Shining*. He was just venting his frustration at Eva's shutting him out. The moment passed and later they were behaving towards each other as if nothing had happened.

Technically Summerhill is a boarding school, but it has little resemblance to the traditional notion of boarding schools. No-one wears uniforms. The children swear freely without fear of being told off. Adolescent couples wander around with their arms round each other. Small children weave around small groups of talking adults, totally involved in their own play, no-one telling them to walk, not run or to not get so excited. Summerhill has often been a focus of media attention, where it is generally portrayed it as the "do-as-you-like school" where unruly children run wild. But there is a lot more to Summerhill than sensation-seeking journalists, who have spent little more than a couple of hours there, would have us believe.

Summerhill was founded in 1921 by A. S. Neill, a Scottish teacher, after he became disillusioned by conventional schooling methods. He saw these methods as a way of breaking the child's will, rather than supporting the process of learning. Neill was influenced by psychoanalysis, which had introduced the then radical notion of the unconscious, and by seeing many of the children he taught going off to be senselessly slaughtered in the First World War. He sought to create an environment in which children could be as possible to be themselves. Motivated by the belief that children are essentially "good" by nature, he

A.S. NEILL SOUGHT TO CREATE AN ENVIRONMENT IN WHICH CHILDREN COULD BE AS FREE AS POSSIBLE TO BE THEMSELVES

IT MAY COME AS A SURPRISE THAT SUMMERHILL HAS MANY LAWS, 200 OR MORE AT A TIME

considered this "goodness" was warped by adult attempts to mould the child into unnatural ways of being. The "goodness" Neill proposed was not the naïve, sentimental innocence that so-many adults attribute to children, but an innate capacity to develop into emotionally open and socially responsible individuals. It was freedom, he declared, that allowed children to stay in touch with and grow in accordance with their inherent "goodness".

Neill maintained his championing of freedom for children until his death in 1973. Fifty years of experience did not change his mind. Summerhill continues today to embody the same principles that it did then and is run by Neill's daughter, Zoë Readhead. It is located, as it was for most of Neill's life, on the outskirts of the small town of Leiston, in Suffolk. Very much an international community, Summerhill draws children from all over the world. It is a small school, with less than a hundred pupils, aged roughly between seven and seventeen. Most of the children board, though some of the younger ones are "day kids" and go home at night. When I was living at the school I was the houseparent for the ten to twelve year olds. Neill dubbed this age group the "gangster age" as they often arrived new at the school having been in mainstream education long enough to have built up a full steam of resentment and rebellion within themselves. Neill sometimes took on quite difficult and disturbed children and allowed freedom to do its work on them. He observes in his books how they began to soften as they resolved their conflicts in the context of a tolerant and easy-going community. I saw the same process at work in my time there. Children whose difficulties would have been compounded by trying to force them to conform to the conventional system of punishments and rewards, became relaxed and sociable with a little time and patience from the community. But I don't want to give the impression that these young "gangsters" are a particularly troubled bunch.

SUMMERHILL TODAY IS RUN BY A.S
NEILL'S DAUGHTER, ZOE. IT IS A SMALL
SCHOOL WITH 70-100 PUPILS

AT SUMMERHILL KIDS ARE FULLY INVOLVED IN THE RULE-MAKING PROCESS

Even the children who were most "well-behaved" in their previous schools, once the pressure was off, allowed aspects of themselves, that had hitherto been kept under wraps to come to the surface. In doing so I saw them become more rounded and confident in themselves.

MAKING AND BREAKING LAWS

I t may then come as a surprise that Summerhill has many rules, or "laws" as they are called. There may be 200 or more such laws at any time. These laws are not dictated by adults, but are proposed and voted on in regular community meetings, in which everyone, adult and child alike, have one vote. The voice of a seven-year-old had equal weight as that of the Principal. In most schools and homes children learn only how to break the rules, not how to make them. At Summerhill the children are fully involved in the whole process and therefore understand and appreciate the reasoning behind the laws. When a community of children sit down to decide the parameters by which they are going to live, they make practical laws based on experience and in relationship. For example, if the smaller children are running around the dining room when the older children are trying to eat, someone may propose that they are not allowed in at that time. Or if some of the twelve-year-olds are putting pressure on the younger children to borrow things and the younger children are finding it difficult to say no, someone may propose a law saying there has to be one of the older kids or an adult present to make sure no pressure is being exerted. Children do not propose or vote for laws based on abstract codes of conduct, such as everyone needs to hold their knife and fork in a certain way or wear a certain style of dress. They naturally come to distinguish between what Neill called "freedom and licence". Freedom is doing what you want as long as it does not interfere with someone else. Licence is doing what you want without caring about the consequences.

THE CHILDREN NATURALLY COME TO DISTINGUISH BETWEEN FREEDOM AND LICENCE

The popular notion is that left to their own devices children will throw all caution to the wind and chaos will prevail. Experience at Summerhill does not bear this out. On one occasion when I was living at the school, we had a lot of new pupils straight out of mainstream education, ready to flex their democratic muscles in the meeting. This was at a time when we had more than the usual number of young children and after a large group of adolescents, who had grown up being part of the law making process and knew their value, had left. Having a strong majority this bunch of new pupils threw out all the laws, with the exception of a handful of health and safety laws that are not open to the meeting. Certainly it was chaotic for a while, with no bedtimes and children riding bicycles up and down the corridors. But within days the community started to vote the laws back in, as they felt the need for them, and by the end of term nearly all the laws were back in place. This experience taught these children that these laws were not just arbitrary and authoritarian, but were there for a reason.

Of course, like anywhere else, the laws get broken all the time, but anyone who wants to has recourse to the meetings to ask for something to be done about it. For example, if someone uses another person's bike without asking, that person can bring a case against the offending individual in the meeting. The person who took the bike can offer an explanation as to why he or she did so and, a vote is taken on whether or not they should be fined. This may just be a strong warning not to do it again, or a small money fine, or to go to the back of the lunch queue. In my experience the community is generally good-natured and fair when it comes to fines. The few individuals who called for heavier fines were always the moralists with bad consciences of their own. Through their use of the meetings the children learn practical boundaries rooted in personal interaction. These are not incomprehensible orders barked at them by bigger people, as many children experience in their lives. Nor is there the lack of clarity that comes when the boundaries are not there, either through neglect or from parents who are afraid of confrontation. Meeting the "no" of others, as long as it is reasonable and can be mutual, gives us the sense of self and other we need to form healthy relationships.

One of the things I always appreciated about the meetings, was the lack of resentment when things did not always go the way people wanted. I remember once bringing a case against a group of big adolescent boys who had been making noise in the night, in an area of the school that they were not meant to be in. This was the culmination of a series of occasions I had been woken up in the night and I argued for a substantial fine. They argued just as passionately against it. But this time the meeting went in my favour and they were fined. As the meeting closed and they filed past me, each of them gave me a big hug and apologised for waking me up. There was no resentful sulking or left over tension, either on their part or mine.

TIME TO PLAY

Another aspect of Summerhill that people often find hard to comprehend is that that lessons are not compulsory. Children only go to lessons when they decide they are ready to learn. People often argue "I would have never learnt anything if I hadn't been made to." My reply would be "Of course not, your desire to learn was killed in you by that very act of being made to." Part of my present work involves teaching adults and, even though they want to learn, I see how much fear they bring with them to the learning process. Compulsory education has undermined their capacity to inquire and replaced it with an anxiety-based need to get it right. Their nervous systems reverberate with the fear of being seen as stupid, instead of resting in the open, receptive state that is conducive to taking in and processing new information. This is a real handicap for many adults and a direct result of the way they have been educated.

When Summerhill children do go to class they tend to learn quite quickly, as they are motivated. They have been able to play as much as they like and are ready to engage with some structured input. Most children do not get enough time to play and be in their own worlds, so find it hard to concentrate at school. They become bored, restless or anxious. Neill declared that if the emotions are free the intellect will look after itself. Certainly as I reflect on the children I was houseparent for, who are now in their mid to late twenties, they all seem to be doing very well in their respective careers. Most went on to further education and now have degrees in a variety of different subjects, some very academic, some more artistic. I have met a broad range of

SUMMERHILL KIDS TEND TO LEARN QUICKLY BECAUSE THEY ARE MOTIVATED

ex-Summerhillians over the years, spanning the whole 85 years of the school's existence, and few wished that they had been made to go to lessons. For the most part they seem to feel that they were really able to develop their own interests and leave Summerhill feeling equipped and ready for the wider world. They also cite other qualities that they feel they got from being at Summerhill, which could not be reaped in the classroom, but developed out of the sense of freedom and community.

THE SUMMERHILL
APPROACH TO
EDUCATION HAS
NOT GENERALLY
SAT WELL WITH
GOVERNMENT
INSPECTORS

So what are these? One is confidence. I see this already in Eva, even though she has only been at Summerhill for two terms and was quite happy in her previous school. She is more relaxed in herself, which allows her to be more outgoing. Another is self-motivation. Not having been organised into endless activities by anxious adults, afraid that their children will not develop into budding violin virtuosos or become multi-lingual before their brain cells dry up or, God forbid, be bored for half an hour, their inner worlds have remained spacious and intact enough for them to know what they want out of life and what they have to offer. During my stint as houseparent I often remember hearing back from an employer or college how much they appreciated the capacity of this or that ex-pupil to engage with work creatively without needing to be told what to do all the time. Another quality that was often remarked on was that of being able to get on with people. Learning to live with people evolves naturally in the life of the community. Ex-Summerhillians, in my experience, are generally very tolerant. They do not judge people by external status symbols, such as clothes, career or wealth. They relate to people primarily as people and are not judgemental of their flaws and struggles.

TAKING ON THE GOVERNMENT

These qualities are not ones that we can measure and award qualifications for. As such they fall outside the criteria of a good education, as laid down by the educational establishment. Education has become highly standardised, with specific goals being set for specific ages. These have to be tested for and pupils' progress measured in terms of good test results. The Summerhill approach to education has not generally sat well with the government inspectors. The attitude of Ofsted (Office for Standards in Education) towards Summerhill has been akin to that of Uncle Vernon's red-faced indignation at the mention of Hogwarts School in the Harry Potter stories. Throughout Neill's career he was always fearful for Summerhill's future, citing only one inspector who ever seemed to grasp what Summerhill was actually about. During the 1990s the inspections started to become more frequent and aggressive, until eventually the school was threatened with closure if it did not bring in measures that would essentially bring an end to non-compulsory lessons.

This culminated in March 2000 in a High Court appeal in which Summerhill challenged the government's formal notice of complaint. It soon became clear that the government inspector's report was full of inaccuracies and prejudices that could not be substantiated in court. It also emerged, that despite the inspectors' assurances that Summerhill was not being specifically targeted, it was on a secret list of schools "to be watched". The government quickly backed down and David Blunkett, the then Minister of Education, offered a set of conciliatory proposals. To quote *The Times* (Friday March 24th 2000): "In extraordinary scenes at the Royal Court of Justice, the school was allowed to take over Court 40 to hold a student council to debate Mr Blunkett's new proposals." Just like any other proposal, the meeting voted on whether to accept David Blunkett's proposals. Essentially these proposals represented a complete turnaround and for the first time in Summerhill's history Neill's educational philosophy came under the protection of the law. It was the end of a long campaign in which the children had been active throughout. They had taken on the British government and won.

For myself, and many others, it is a great relief that this one small school that champions children's freedom has been able to survive. This is personal—it is my daughter's school, she chose to go there and I was able to and happy to support her in this. It is also a part of my personal history: Summerhill remains for me the strongest sense of community that I have experienced in my life. But it is also the living embodiment of a way of raising children that forces us to think about the fear-based way in which children are so often regarded: fear that if we do not force them they will not learn. Fear that if we do not mould them they will go rotten. Fear that at our core there is a badness that needs to be made good. If there is one thing that Summerhill offers us it is that we do not need to be so afraid. ◉

Matthew Appleton is the author of A Free Range Childhood: Self Regulation at Summerhill School *published by Gale Centre Publications*

Leave Them Alone!

TOM HODGKINSON **HAS SOME TIPS ON CHILDCARE FOR IDLERS. ILLUSTRATIONS BY** HANNAH DYSON

First of all let me say that I am in no way writing from a position of smugosity. I have three children under the age of seven, love them all, but they also drive me *completely insane* at times. If anything, this article is a record of the mistakes I have made, with a few reflections on how to make things easier, or at least more enjoyable, in the future. Or I should say, from now.

As an idler with three small children, people say to me: looking after children is not very idle. Well, no. In many senses it is not. You have to get up at seven or earlier. Nights are broken. Children make an unbelievable amount of mess so you are constantly cleaning up. They have to be bathed, fed, clothed, put on the school bus and collected from friends' houses. They whine. However, we as a society in recent years have made things much more difficult for ourselves, and much more difficult than they need to be, by applying a work ethic to childhood. Children these days seem to be endlessly busy. Where we have jobs, children are expected to have umpteen "activities". Ballet, tennis lessons, music class. Every day they are being trained in something or other rather than just being left to play. A woman I met on holiday once said how much she hated this phrase "art project" that gets bandied around. Why can't they just muck around? Why the rampant over-scheduling, with all the extra work it involves for parents? What happened to play?

Now, before moving on to my tips for responsible parenting, which to me is synonymous with idle parenting, I would like to explain the intellectual philosophy that I've based the tips on. It comes from the following lines from an essay called "Education of the People", written in 1918 by DH Lawrence, and published today in the anthology *Phoenix*:

How to begin to educate a child. First rule, leave him alone. Second rule, leave him alone. Third rule, leave him alone. That is the whole beginning.

My friend the great *Guardian* columnist Slack Dad was much struck, as you might well believe, by these lines, when I showed them to him last year. We were sitting on a grassy knoll, drinking and trying to ignore our children, so you can see the appeal.

DH Lawrence is absolutely right. There is far too much interference in the lives of children. This interference is usually carried out under the excuse of "Health and Safety". Oh Health and Safety, thou monstrous two-headed enemy to Liberty! How many crimes to humanity have been committed in thy name? I understand, for example, that in nursery schools around the country, which are now known by the unappealing term "pre-schools", running around is not allowed. Running around not allowed! For children of three and four? Surely they should be doing nothing but running around! But no. We have decided somewhere along the line that three-year olds should be prepared for the discipline of school in pre-schools, where their natural urges will begin to be tamed. Interference sometimes goes under another name: education. Apparently pre-schools have an educational remit. Why? Kids should be free to run wild. The best pre-school would be a large room with garden attached, twenty kids and two adults at one end ignoring them.

Now Lawrence was not of course recommending slothful neglect. We don't let our children eat nails. What he meant was that we should allow them space, physical and mental. "It is this in respect that we repeat, leave him alone. Leave his sensibilities, his emotions, his spirit, and his mind severely alone." The "leave them alone" philosophy, or "benign neglect" as it is sometimes called, seems in direct opposition to everything that we have decided to believe. You are supposed to play with children, give them attention, give them "special time", "mummy time", "quality time". You are asked to make "play dates". Thus it is that childcare becomes a burdensome task rather than a pleasure. We are taught by TV supernannies how to look after our children. Now supernanny has lots of good tips, but she can end up making us feel like bad parents because we're extremely unlikely to be able to live up to the high standards she exhibits. Well, if you don't feel like it, don't do it. It's surely worse, for example, to play a game with your kid under sufferance, resenting every second, than to ignore them and read the paper while they find something to do. "Bill, play with Fred", I heard a mother command her husband, in relation to their son. "I thought play was supposed to be a spontaneous thing", came the lugubrious reply. Now of course, we all do play with our kids, but to do it on command and at pre-appointed times defeats the object.

When we over-schedule and over-stimulate our kids, and conform them to the clock, we don't leave enough to their own imaginations, to their own resources. We will make them resourceless. They will come to rely on pre-organised "activities" without acting for themselves. I think of the great *New Yorker* cartoon which satirised this work-ethic trend in parenting. Two children are standing next to each other, both staring at their Palm Pilots. "Well," says one to the other. "I can fit you in for unscheduled play next Thursday at four." This we may call the Doctrine of Activities and it is to be avoided for both your sakes.

With our eldest son we definitely made the mistake of over-stimulating him when he was small, whether playing with him or letting him watch lots of TV. We were in his face. "*I... need... some... entertainment!*" he bellowed the other day. Already he is in danger of becoming a passive consumer of entertainment, rather than a creator, a player. The younger two have been more left alone, simply because there wasn't time to give them the same amount of attention as number one, and the result is that both are showing signs of being more self-sufficient, more able to look after their own selves.

It's amazing how resourceful children are, once given the opportunity, once left alone. The other day, in a fit of pious rage, I stormed into the sitting room and turned the television off. To be sure,

OH, HEALTH AND SAFETY! HOW MANY CRIMES AGAINST HUMANITY HAVE BEEN COMMITTED IN THY NAME!

they objected at first. But soon they were playing their own games. Later I realized that I was washing up while all three of them played near me in the kitchen, without hassling me! How I achieved this miracle, I don't know, but I suspect it was by leaving them alone. By leaving them alone, also, I have discovered, it is even possible to do something enjoyable like read while you are looking after them. Carry a book around with you to take out at odd moments. Yesterday I even managed to have a short nap on the sofa while the baby played around me on the floor. Henry is now playing next door as I write this.

The "leave them alone" philosophy is better for the kids and less work for the grown-ups. If kids grow up accustomed to looking after themselves, then they will surely turn into resourceful and independent adults who do not look for external agencies such as employers or governments or commercialised entertainment systems to sort their lives out for them. They will be like the Famous Five, the Narnia children, Wendy, John and Michael in *Peter Pan,* Harry Potter, the Baudelaire orphans: parentless and free.

A key element of idle parenting is to get the kids to work for you. They seem to quite enjoy it. My friend John will lie in a hammock and command his daughter to bring him beer, Rizlas and tobacco. Arthur has taken to making porridge in the morning while we lie in. Soon he'll be bringing us tea. You see the positive effects of leaving them alone?

We should perhaps even leave them alone when they fight, rather than rushing over to tell them off the moment one hits the other. For whatever reason, children do hit each other. They just do. It is something they will grow out of when they realise that there are less painful ways of settling disputes. Certainly however much we tell them not to hit each other, they continue. Hitting may even be seen as a sign of refusal to accept submission. Indeed, we should be inspired by the natural imperious spirit of children, and by their passion and zest for life.

> WE SHOULD BE INSPIRED BY THE NATURAL IMPERIOUS SPIRIT OF CHILDREN AND BY THEIR PASSION AND ZEST FOR LIFE

ANOTHER TRICK THAT WORKS IS TO COMBINE DRINKING WITH CHILDCARE

Leaving them alone also works in the case of bad behaviour. When you feel you are about to lose your temper, simply walk out of the room. Ignore the tantrums as far as you possibly can. This is one are where I would concur with supernanny: ignore the bad behaviour. Kids are little drama queens: their zest for life displays itself in tantrums, as well as fun and laughter and silliness. The more we avoid feeding the hissy-fits, by telling them off, the sooner they will be over.

In my ideal world I would also give the kids far fewer toys, particularly the plastic ones with five million bits that get lost or have to be cleared up. The best toy, I have often thought, would be a block of wood. Nothing to lose, nothing to break and not too offensive to the parents' aesthetic sense either. A simple block of wood can also be transformed into anything by the child's imagination. In fact, one episode of *The Simpsons* featured a TV advert for a toy called "Log!" which was, simply, a log. The joke, of course, was the ingenious way that marketing men have of packaging something without value and making it into a special toy with a price tag. But still, Log. I thought that was a good idea.

When it comes to toys, baby Henry seems to get more pleasure from a wooden spoon and a saucepan than from the brightly-coloured educational toys with batteries that run out that we give him.

Having said all that, we got a lot of pleasure from Arthur's remote control Dalek. Although I notice that he hasn't played with it since the 30th of December, and the blimmin' thing cost forty quid.

One trick that makes life easier is to combine things that you like doing with the things that they like doing. An example of this is making things in the workshop. They seem to really enjoy getting nails and handing me hammers, and playing amongst the mess and rubble. And I am doing something useful, like making a bench.

Another trick that works is to combine drinking with childcare. Drinking makes you less grumpy (albeit temporarily) and less inclined to impose mind forg'd dualities like good and bad. It also loosens the hold of the internal Puritan and kids respond well to that.

Getting other children over to play makes your life easier, because they play with each other and leave you alone, and it gives the other parent a break. The children are happiest when with friends. Indeed, one problem that we all face is the nuclear family and the lack of neighbourliness. Four people squashed together in a house and told to get on with it with only the TV for guidance is not a natural situation. The TV has replaced Granny, sitting in the corner and minding the kids while Mum gets on with housework. It's no wonder we find things tough. So you need to live in a quiet street of terraced houses, with lots of other familes in a similar situation. Then the other kids will pop round and play. I grew up in this sort of set-up and we would be out in the streets all day. Now I live in the country and I really wish we had one or two families with small children living in our tiny village, but there are none. So instead we invite friends to come and stay. That seems to ease the burden: the more adults there are, the better, as well as the more children. When I lived in the city we had a wonderful lodger, and his presence made us all behave a little better. The adults also need adult company.

The other tip is always, always, always get enough sleep. The terrible cruelty of young children is the sleep deprivation they impose on their parents. The answer is for both parents to do as little work as possible in the first two years, to enable lots of extra time for naps. Perhaps both parents could take part-time jobs, leaving more time for naps and for hanging around at home. And two three-day-a-week jobs add up to slightly more money, in theory, than one full-time job. So it is a better solution than "Mum stays at home, Dad works". Or work out a way of both of you working from home. If this is impossible, then make sure you go to bed early. That sounds like pious advice from the *Idler*, but it's better to go to bed at nine and feel awake the next day than wander round in a mist of grumpiness because you haven't had enough sleep.

One final bugbear I'd like to mention is the Doctrine of Consistency. "As long as you're consistent," they say, "it doesn't matter what your rules are." Well, Hitler was consistent, wasn't he? Consistency is evil and in any case, impossible. In the family, how can you possibly be consistent? Every day is different. Partners accuse each other of having "mood swings". Well of course you have bloody mood swings, otherwise you'd be a bleedin' robot. The drive towards consistency is only ever going to make us feel bad because we will inevitably be inconsistent. Sometimes you are going to sit round the table together and eat dinner. At other times you might sit on the floor and have a picnic. If you only ever do one and never change the routine then things are going to get mighty boring. It is humanly impossible to be consistent.

So our low-effort approach to childcare seems to have three definite advantages: one, it is easier than trying to keep them entertained all the time, two, it is cheaper, and three, it produces more confident children who are able to look after themselves and will not constantly seek a parent-substitute in later life, whether that be employer or spouse. The idling approach is cheap, easy and effective. Minimize authority and maximize freedom, that should be our plan. And "leave them alone" our mantra. ☻

The Cons of Pros

ROB WESTWOOD DECLARES WAR ON THE BIZARRE
AND DAMAGING CULT OF THE PROFESSIONAL.
ILLUSTRATIONS BY B.P. PERRY

Working as an office functionary a few summers ago for a local university, I was handed a report by my supervisor as part of a performance review. According to the report, my work in the office had been "first class", with the wider implication that I was performing as a respectable member of society at last. Dad would be so chuffed. There was however, one caveat:

"Rob's laid-back, accessible attitude has allowed him to gel well with his colleagues and to fit into the system. He should be advised, however, that in some institutes, his laid-back approach to work may be considered unprofessional."

Unprofessional? But I had never claimed to be a professional. I held no professional qualification, nor was I a member of any professional body. I'd not even held down a job that could be considered a professional one. I was just some kid.

What the hell is professionalism anyway? What is this vague thing that's supposed to determine all workplace behaviour? It is surely important to understand how the professional mechanism works, given that it permeates every aspect of work culture from staffroom to sales floor. But surprisingly, the disciplines of organisational psychology, sociology and business management have very little to say about it. The anarchist philosopher Bob Black writes: "[All ideologies, left- or right-wing] will carry on endlessly about wages, hours, working conditions, exploitation, productivity, profitability. They'll gladly talk about anything but work itself." Indeed it seems to be assumed that professionalism is an intrinsically good thing (or else one without a conceptualised alternative) and so hardly anyone seems to have cast a critical eye over the topic.

In order to try to find some half-decent definition of the nebulous thing that dictates our workplace etiquette, I decided to look to the philosophers. While many of these guys lived and died before the modern incarnation of the word "professional" was even invented, their work provides an underlying matrix to the way that organisation works.

PROFESSIONALISM IS MANIPULATIVE, PRETENTIOUS AND INDIVIDUALISING. NO WONDER SO MANY DIE FROM WORK-RELATED STRESS DISORDERS

Bob Black points out that to define work ("Compulsory Production") is to despise it and I discovered something similar when I sought to define professionalism. When one gains a clearer image of where professionalism comes from and what its function is, it is quite difficult not to hate it. It is a manipulative, pretentious and individualising technology, incapable of avoiding social segregation. No wonder so many people die from work-related stress disorders.

David Brent, the managerial boob portrayed by Ricky Gervais in *The Office*, preaches in one episode of the sitcom that "Professionalism is... and that's what I want." He reveals that he has not even the vaguest idea of what professionalism is, which is probably why he spends most of his time playing around with "Big Mouth Billy Bass". Brent is an accidental anarchist and champion of unprofessionalism. But maybe his "Professionalism is..." sentence can be completed after a little rumination.

PROFESSIONALISM IS... PANOPTICONIC

A panopticon is the name given to the architectural design of a prison building conceived of by the utilitarian philosopher, Jeremy Bentham. It consists of a cylindrical or circular building like an amphitheatre with a single watchtower in the centre, occupied by one guard. The inward-facing windows of the main building are tinted so that the guard can see into each cell but so the prisoners cannot see out to the guard. The blackened windows become symbolic of the guard's supervision and the inmates must assume that they are constantly being watched—it is a near-perfect system of government in which the one can govern the many.

In his 1975 book, *Discipline and Punish*, the postmodern thinker Michel Foucault uses the panopticon as a metaphor for how society is self-regulatory, how a culture of fear has been engineered and how the privileged few are in control of the oppressed many. Professionalism, too, I believe, is a technology not entirely unlike Bentham's panopticon.

One of the key aspects of panopticism is that it separates its subjects. Bentham, in his 1843 plans of the panopticon prison system explains that the inmates are supervised "by a sequestered and observed solitude". And of the cells Foucault writes: "They are like so many cages, so many small theatres, in which each actor is alone, perfectly individualised and constantly visible", and that "the major effect of the panopticon [is] to induce in the inmate a state of conscious and permanent visibility that assures the automatic functioning of power".

When this is applied to the workplace, and we replace the idea of inmates with workers, then, as Foucault writes, "there are no disorders, no theft, no coalitions, none of those distractions that slow down the rate of work, make it less perfect or cause accidents."

Professionalism in the form of job descriptions, wage scale and level of training is the workplace version of panopticonic technology. In an automobile factory, if there is a problem with the windscreen wipers of the final product, then the one guy who makes the windscreen wipers can be isolated and blamed. So everyone must focus upon their own part of the task out of the threat that they will be caught out as being a fraud or a slacker.

If the guard were to take a prolonged bathroom break or decide not to come into work one day, the prisoners would still maintain obedience. In professionalism, though the architect of the system is long dead, the majority of people continue to observe his authority and so the system of self-regulation goes on and on.

While working at the same university I mentioned at the beginning of the article, it was explained to me that the institute goes through an annual quiet spell: during the summer, the majority of students have little to study for and so there is less demand upon the staff. So finding jobs for every member of the "team" would be a difficult task for the supervisors to implement. There was an unspoken understanding between the supervisors and the staff that we must not work too hard or too quickly, since there were only so many jobs to go around and it wouldn't "look good" in the eyes of the deceased architect to have people sitting idle.

And this, perhaps, is one of my key arguments against professionalism. When we understand that the architect is dead and that we perform only to memories of memories of his surveillance—to his out-of-time and no-longer-manned sentinels—we must give up the ghost or continue to suffer the consequences.

PRETENCE

Professionalism is employed as an untrue aesthetic and calls upon us to falsify personalities. It essentially invents what Thomas Hobbes called "artificial" or "feigned" people. Hobbes notes in his famous 1651 publication *Leviathan* that the word "person" derives from the Latin persona: a character portrayed on stage by an actor. And just as an actor acts, so do people in the professional context. Hobbes writes: "Of Persons Artificiall, some have their words and actions owned by those whom they represent. And then the person is the Actor; and he that owneth [the actor's] words and actions, is the Author: In which case the actor acteth by Authority."

He goes on to say that the only people who act under authority without their own sense of reason are "Children, Fooles and Mad-men". Which are you, boy?

This problem is illustrated beautifully by Jean-Paul Sartre in his 1943 doorstop of a book, *Being and Nothingness*. He describes a waiter whose behaviour in the café is purely theatrical: "his movement is quick and forward, a little too precise" and "his eyes express an interest a little too solicitous for the order of the customer" So what is up with this guy? Sartre explains: "He is playing at being a waiter in a café."

When he leaves the café after his shift, he ceases to be a waiter and returns to what Hobbes would call his "natural self". So why the need for professional falsehood? Sartre explains it as a battle between facticity and transcendence: the professional "waiter" part of the man competing with his "free" and human side.

The real individual behind the persona is not the person required for the café job, for the true person required for the job can only be the waiter's employer: the employer after all is the one who wants to get food on the tables and to put money in the till. But the employer is lazy or otherwise engaged and so the employee must act as an agent and perform the master's deeds in his absence. The waiter does not want to wait; he simply has to be there in order to earn his wages with which to buy food and drink. So he is running the errands of the managers: acting out the pre-prepared script just as the employer desires and just as the actor does on stage. Moreover, by acting and not truly entering the spirit of things, he is removing himself from any consequences of his actions: he is, as the old war criminals say, only obeying orders.

How long can this madness go on? How long can a whole society go on pretending to be people they aren't just so that they can go on paying the rent. Kurt Vonnegut, a true philosopher if ever there was one, writes in his novel *Mother Night* that "We are what we pretend to be so we must be careful what we pretend to be." And he's absolutely right. People can surely not live on pretence alone and when we're not actually engaged in work and cowering behind our professional personas, we are recovering from them or preparing to put them on.

INSTRUMENTAL IN CREATING SOCIAL RIFTS

The assumption that social rifts are categorically bad derives from the "Five Steps to Tyranny" idea proposed in the 1990s by the psychologist, Stanley Milgram. "Tyranny" refers to the path to an all-out final war and the end of civilisation; the first step on which is the forming of social rifts caused by a hatred or fear of "difference" as opposed to the celebration of "diversity". It is happening all around us already in the arenas of race, sexuality, gender and religion and professionalism isn't helping things either.

From looking at the panopticonic nature of professionalism alone, we can see that social rifts are unavoidable in that the ultimate shattering of a collective takes place as a result of individualising measures.

Rifts occur due to the identification (or invention) of in-groups and out-groups. In professional organisations, there is an undeniable rift between managers and staff where staff consider the various levels of management to be the stuff of out-groups and vice versa. Even this article has positioned managers and employers as being the bad guys in that managers are the ones who serve as guards in the panopticon without much in the way of a quibble, and employers the ones who bring about the problem of agency or pretence.

But neither managers nor staff are inhuman out-groups: outside of the workplace both managers and staff are unranked, unprofessionalised humans. It is only within the organisation that humans are divided into masters and slaves. Management/Staff or Masters/Slaves is the most obvious example of segregation caused by professionalism. Professional underlings are sick and tired of managers riding their backs: they are oversupervised, underpaid and not given the credit or respect they have been promised by the universally naïve understanding of professionalism. Managers, on the other hand, are fed up with underlings not working to their full potential, stealing from stock, grumbling about their workloads and questioning authority. Hence the rift. But the rift is only a product of professionalism, for it is seen to be professional for a company to have a hierarchy of managers and staff.

A THORN IN THE SIDE OF BOTH WORK AND PLAY

Anarchist philosopher, Bob Black is quite insistent that work is bad for your health: "Work is the source of nearly all the misery in the world," he writes. "Almost any evil you'd care to name comes from working or from living in a world designed for work. In order to stop suffering, we have to stop working."

Such buoyancy is difficult to argue with, isn't it? But where Black's famous 1985 essay, "The Abolition of Work" explains how work is the cause of any social ill you care to name, I'd argue that it's not "work" per se but professionalism that causes the misery and suffering.

Black subscribes to what he calls a Ludic Conviviality: the idea that play is more productive and satisfying and worthy of human attention than work. He writes: "Play isn't passive. Doubtless we all need a lot more time for sheer sloth and slack than we ever enjoy now, regardless of income or occupation, but once recovered from employment-induced exhaustion nearly all of us want to act."

Play, Black argues, is not without consequence. It's just that the consequence does not happen at the end of the process as with work, and mostly in the grubby hands of someone else, but rather along the way. He writes that in a Ludic Utopia, "life will become a game, or rather many games, but not—as it is now—a zero/sum game. An optimal sexual encounter is the paradigm of productive play, The participants potentiate each other's pleasures, nobody keeps score, and everybody wins. The more you give, the more you get. In the ludic life, the best of sex will diffuse into the better part of daily life."

But imagine a professional variation of play. Imagine play confined to specified etiquette and with hierarchies where the microphysics of power are conducted just as they are in the workplace. It would suck. It would essentially be work given that the outcome would not be gratuitous. So it is not necessarily "work" that is bad, for one can assuredly enjoy many modes of work. Work can be rewarding: it can provide direction in life; can help to support worthy organisations; or can allow you to appreciate the good things in life which would be more trivial without the contrasting hardship. In the sex example, one body can "work" to stimulate the erogenous zones of the other and that will most likely be fun: it is work as its own reward. This can only occur after the removal of the professional dimension.

I'm confident when I say that an elimination of professionalism and a promotion of work-as-play will allow individuals to exist as genuine human people rather than as Hobbesian parodies. As a result we can lead happier, more fulfilled and possibly even —mercy me—more productive lives. By extension, I'm certain that a programme of "deprofessionalisation" would allow organisations to prosper and grow. Modern companies were invented by professionalism and fashioned to be strange machines existing between people rather than as people.

An alternative to professionalism is, I propose, "collegiality": a structure of peers in which people can work with other people towards common goals without questionable authority, persona or pretence. When the error of professionalism has been recognised and amended, things can begin to improve. ☺

Art of the Nap

PHOTOGRAPHS BY GILES GODWIN

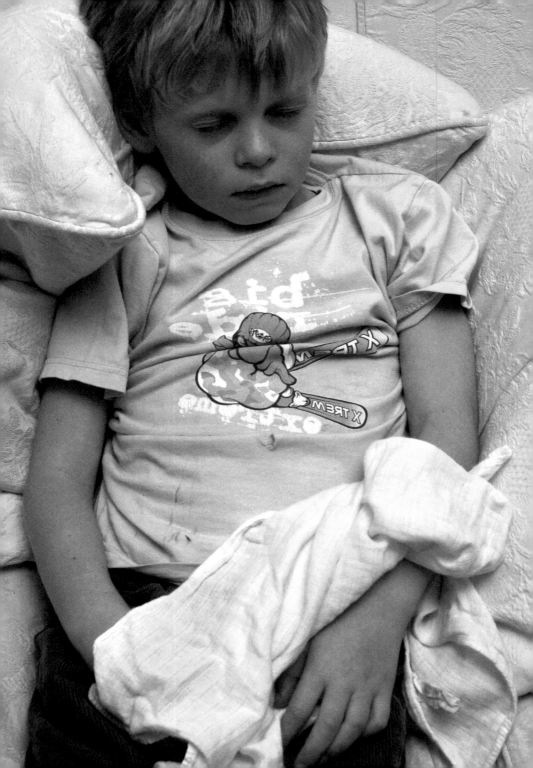

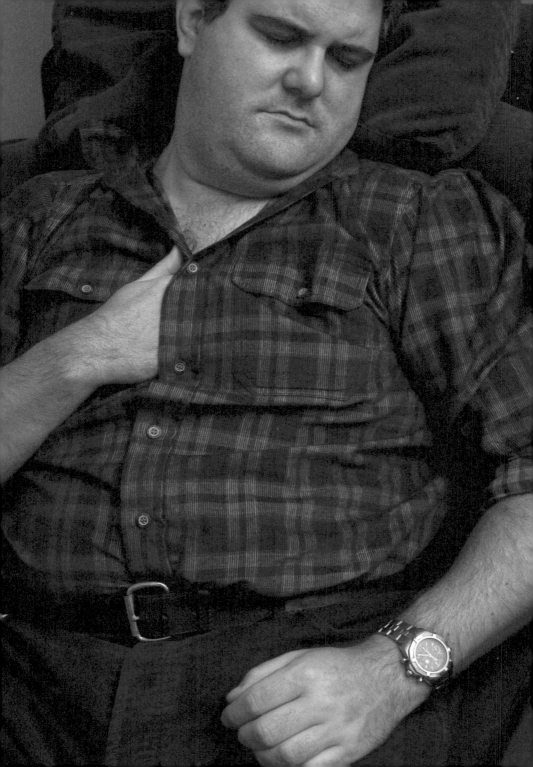

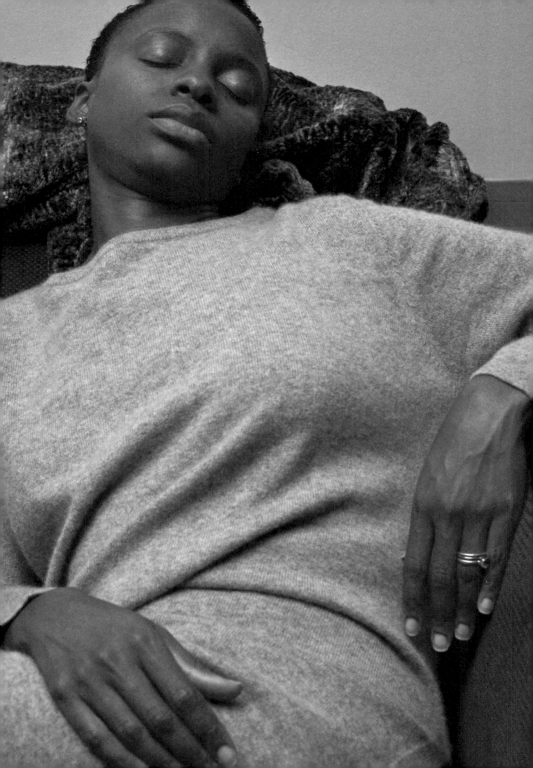

CHILD BEATING
AS A HUMOROUS
AID TO SELL
STOVES

Little Devils

EVIL OR INNOCENT? JOHN NICHOLSON ON HOW
CHILDREN BECAME SEEN NOT AS CAREFREE SOULS
WHO WERE LEFT ALONE BUT AS EVIL TOTS IN NEED
OF SALVATION AND TRAINING

*As innocent as children seem to be to us… they are young vipers, and are infinitely more
hateful than vipers… They are naturally very senseless and stupid…
and need much to awaken them*
American clergyman, 18th century

"**W**omen and children first!" Rather than calling for priority for the prime trouble-makers to perish, sentimentality triumphed over the view of women and children as the root of all evil. Instead a fake chivalric ideal exhorts us to protect and save those least able to look after themselves. Admirable, although a contradiction of "the survival of the fittest" principle unless you see this selfless act as a way of safeguarding the race.

Casting women and children in such a transcendent role runs contrary to most previous views in all cultures and taints attitudes to this day. The word of a child is accepted over the adult in cases of accusation. The child is innocent, the adult is presumed guilty. Children can do no wrong.

Certainly the opposite view, that children can do no right, prevailed in the days when floggers and caners laid into brats or while believers in Original Sin exorcised babies at the font. Doors were built into churches for the evil spirits to escape from the baptised tot.

A by-product was the genre which contrasted the good and bad child. Yet this raises profound questions, since the concepts were unknown until recently in our culture. In 15th century books of hours and church triptychs children are regularly shown in acts which are now condemned, in street scenes they expose themselves, urinate, are breast-fed and even circumcised as other children and adults nearby can see. These scenes are not treated as remarkable but part of the physical world common to every class and every age group.

SEVERE PUNISHMENT FOR BOYS WAS THOUGHT SO BENEFICIAL
THE ODD MURDER BY A SCHOOLMASTER WAS WORTH IT

"Good" simply meant doing what was expected, fitting in. Children were ignored, left alone. Obedience and innocence were not singled out and a lack of concern covered other natural behaviours such as masturbation. This practice, far from being thought shameful with all the apparatus of guilt, was expected as not only widespread but inevitable. The medieval temperament shared Fallopius's view that masturbation was good since it enlarged the penis.

How differently such matters were viewed by puritanical families, always on guard against the Devil and all his works, as Anita Schorsch writes in her 1979 study, *Childhood Liberty*:

> *Childhood liberty… opened the doors to the evil of children in their natural inherited and rebellious state of sin. Disobedience, the original sin, was the first and most obvious offence to the "representatives of God", their parents. Even the merest look of discontent in performing childhood "duties" signalled an inward "rebellion" and an unwilling resignation, signs that the child did not believe in the sovereignty of God. Disobedience to the father and his authority and consequent disruption of the family sense of order seemed to threaten the very structure of early modern society.*

A pious mother was ever watchful for further signs and quick to stamp out the Devil. The mother of John Wesley was one such zealot. Her regime for child-raising clearly did John no harm as he recommended it to his followers, with knobs on. Susanna Wesley taught her children "to fear the rod and to cry softly". Presumably this was on the grounds that "children should be seen and not heard", rather than any distress their audible pain might cause her.

So children were prime targets for being cured. An armoury of weapons were deployed from the easiest—physical attacks—to tying babies in their cots so they could not move, to imprisoning infants in cages. "The young child which lieth in the cradle is both wayward and full of affections; and though his body be but small, yet he hath a wrong-doing heart, and is altogether inclined to evil. If this sparkle be suffered to increase, it will rage over and burn down the whole house."

Food could be used like a whip, to reward or deprive. Susanna Wesley, again, was in the forefront. "Whatever they had, they were never permitted at those meals to eat more than one thing, and of that sparingly enough. Drinking or eating between meals was never allowed, unless in the case of sickness, which seldom happened. Nor were they suffered to go into the kitchen to ask anything of the servants when they were at meat; if it was known they do so, they were certainly beat, and the servants severely reprimanded."

Her son learned her lesson and passed it on. "Next to self-will and pride," he exclaimed, "the most fateful disease with which we are born, is love of the world." Therefore he insisted that parents who provide a varied diet or, in his words, "enlarge the pleasure of tasting", invited passions which unsettle the character. One commentator translated this to mean: "To discipline the palate and to govern the stomach are important elements in shaping the character of children." No enjoyment was consistent. Instead of fun and games children

TOP: HOME OR
WORKSHOP?
BOTTOM:
LEARNING FROM
MISS WHIPLASH

should steer their passions for thrills towards pious pastimes such as conversations with Christians, reading devotional books, gardening and visiting friends for tea.

Not only as mothers did women have the crucial role but also "benevolent and intelligent" women—often spinsters and so not liable to maternal weakness—who "pined for an opportunity to aid in carrying the Gospel to the destitute" should run schools of instruction along the lines advocated by Susanna Wesley which would assist them in "training our whole race for heaven".

Magnify your office, teacher!
Higher than the kings of earth;—
Are you not the prophet preacher,
To the future giving birth?

The new elect looked for signs everywhere. These were easily expressed as contrasts between good and bad, the old and new. Look how the Catholic Church allowed sin to flourish in children! Look how corrupt their monks were, particularly those parasitic orders which lived as beggars. The self-righteous interpreted *caritas*, charity, very differently. To give alms to the vast army of superfluous and non-productive mouths—the beggars, vagrants, orphans, foundlings, runaways, vagabonds, prostitutes and thieves—was blasphemy. Instead what an opportunity for salvation! For curing and saving souls from the Devil. The idleness of Poverty was the root of the sin that created a bad child.

If they did not reform then either they deserved to die or be shipped out. Inspired by the Act of 1703, the magistrate Sir John Fielding organised a society to fit out and send to sea more than 10,000 boys. Wayward girls—presumably all prostitutes—should learn the value of labour in reformatories, Female Orphan Asylums. These doubled by offering not only commercial services like laundries but a supply of cowed servant girls for respectable households. The "graduates" had been trained to toil and spin, to knit stockings, to make artificial flowers, toys, gloves and carpets. Thus they should be not only "good" but also self-supporting. The streets, and society, should be cleansed of rogues.

These reformatories preceded the Industrial Revolution which is customarily seen in terms of the terrible conditions inflicted on the workers. This overlooks who were the workers. In some mills 50% of the workforce could be children. Indeed a third of all textile workers were "little elves". Childish slacking was blamed for the accidents which were frequent. "They seldom lose the hand, it only takes off fingers at the first or second joint. Sheer carelessness —looking about them—sheer carelessness!"

But bad as the conditions of working children might be in Industry, they were even worse off in the homes and workshops of private families.

The Poor regarded their children not merely as burdensome mouths but as convertible assets and sold thousands of them as slaves to chimney sweeps, mine owners and others. Trading in children was big business. In the countryside, fairs in market towns often included not only hiring markets for labourers but also for

TOP:
SUPERVISION IN
THE FACTORY,
C1840
BOTTOM: CREEPIE
CRAWLIES

children. Young boys were displayed in "bullrings" to farmers. If the terms in factories sound harsh—a child of seven worked from sunrise to sunset six days a week with two and half days off per year—then life in the fields was often tougher.

Is it any wonder this regime produced institutionalised victims, such as this account from a worker in a Massachusetts mill?

The discipline our work brought us was of great value. We were obliged to be in the mill at just such a minute, in every hour, in order to doff our full bobbins and replace them with empty ones. We went to our meals and returned at the same hour every day. We worked and played at regular intervals, and thus our hands became deft, our fingers nimble, our feet swift, and we were taught daily habits of regularity and of industry; it was, in fact, a sort of manual training or industrial school.

Those who escaped the benefits of regular employment and gang masters might find themselves at the mercy of professional beggars. A beggar woman in 1761 got two years in prison for putting out the eyes of her charges to make them more appealing. Teeth were extracted from children and sold for false teeth worn by the rich. The workhouses were barely tolerated since they were seen as universities of crime. Fagin was heir to many real-life child-masters.

Concern was expressed about how children suffered in the factories and mines. But not because of the physical abuse, rather because the conditions would warp young minds. For example, very young children saw adults in a state of undress or nakedness or answering calls of nature. Worse, they lacked education and were found ignorant of essential knowledge such as the Holy Ghost, the Blessed Trinity or even who the queen was. By the end of the 19th century, successive reforms were working. Progressive owners provided "continuation schools" where mill girls learned "domestic science" without pay.

The calculated rings of moral as well as physical imprisonment remind us of the concentration camps with their concentric circles of informants outside the wire. Internal police—conscience—checked on any deviance. The emphasis shifted to being serious, compulsive and industrious. One 18th century commentator saw the Calvinistic drive for children to "be good" as a choice between the "Life of Effeminacy, Indolence and Obscurity, or a Life of Industry, Temperance, and Honour". He warned against the sort of obstacles children could encounter on the path to Righteousness, "Let no Girl, no Gun, no Cards, no flutes, no Violins, no Dress, no Tobacco, no Laziness, decoy you."

Sin! Thunder rumbled from the pulpits of hellfire preachers. As the godly strove to build God's kingdom on earth who could question the universal scourge being applied to children? By their parents, teachers, and in the workplace? "Spare the rod and spoil the child", was the motto which answered tears, cries and any reservations. The traditional preface before a beating, "this is going to hurt me more than it hurts you", was sincere. The torments inflicted on children did not belong to them but amplified the piety of their persecutors. ◉

Angling for Liberty

IN THIS EXTRACT FROM HIS FORTHCOMING
BOOK, HOW TO FISH, CHRIS YATES SEEKS
FREEDOM IN FISHING. PICS BY CHRIS YATES

The Hampton Court perch incident had a kind of precedent. Four years earlier I made a similar but even more outstanding discovery that was also linked to ideas of mystery and freedom, though, until I was marched off for my first day at school, freedom was not a concept I needed to think about and it was only when the school gates closed behind me that I began to appreciate my former carefree existence and understand that freedom would now be denied me until I'd learnt how to earn it. But the more exercise books that pleaded with me to write something, anything, on their blank pages, the more I yearned to escape them—to be free again to explore the world alone or with other boys my age and not be guided by any authoritative hand, to once again find my own way into castles of fallen trees, up mountains of hay bales or over garden walls into other worlds. I also longed to get back to the village pond, a vast expanse of water that I'd only recently circumnavigated in Wellington boots, towing my yacht Endeavour behind me. During the voyage I had naturally kept a wary eye out for sharks and pirates, but couldn't avoid an encounter with a sea monster that was undeniably and palpably real, if not actually of the sea.

What was it? It had risen up out of the green murk, golden, glittering, stupendous—at least twice as long as the Endeavour, and with a fin on its back almost as big as the sail. When I came ashore I asked the local inhabitants if they'd seen it too, but there was only one other who'd witnessed the spectacle and he didn't know what it was, either.

There was a distant island that I'd been trying to reach but the waters around it were too deep and dangerous for my boots. As I looked back towards it, still wobbly after the confrontation, the creature re-appeared, its broad back breaking the surface. Incredibly it was joined by several others,

all equally immense—and this in a pond I'd been paddling around since the day I'd learned to walk, and where no-one had ever before seen anything bigger that a sardine. Splashing and rolling, the giants eventually passed out of sight beneath the forest of willows on the far bank.

For a while afterwards—maybe a week or two—I remained in a state of quiet shock, but then it became necessary to know exactly what kind of creatures they were. Did they have a name? Were they really my own discovery? Did they truly exist or had they just been a trick of the light? I didn't have long enough to find any answers because, shortly afterwards, school closed over me and began to trivialise everything about the world that I'd thought was wonderful, including monsters in ponds.

My early education was concerned mostly with facts and certainties, yet the only fact that mattered to me was that I couldn't see out of the high Victorian windows, and the only certainties that gave me hope was that a bell would ring in the afternoon, the doors would open and I could breathe again. I had never, as I said, thought about freedom or time or space until school took them away from me, but though I could still savour these things

AT THREE O'CLOCK I JUST WANTED TO RUN AND RUN

during my daily parole, there was a new wildness about me then that made me lose my sense of direction. The pressure of six hours confinement meant that, at three o'clock, I just wanted to run and run and run. It was the same with all my friends. There had never been any urgency between us before, but once schooling began we were always in a great hurry to do things whenever we were free again. It was almost as if, having discovered what boredom was, we were determined not to let it affect our own world; but the result was that, instead of quietly following our own paths back to the old magic, we got confused and distracted and so never had enough time to get there. The village pond was only a sixty second run from school, but the new pace of life meant that my patience could never last long enough for the mystery to reveal itself again. I still believed in it, but after a month or two my faith began to waver. So the pond reverted to what it was always good for: a place for throwing stones, for sailing and sinking model boats, for falling into; and the monsters gradually sank down to the same status as the ghost Billy saw in the sweet shop window and the goblin that Dennis chased into the bracken on the heath.

Time moved busily on, corralled more and more into routines, yet the monsters would still occasionally rise up, usually in the middle of lessons, and I'd find myself adding fish instead of numbers. I once had a vague idea that I might ask one of the anglers who occasionally fished the pond whether they'd ever seen anything unusual, but when, eventually, the opportunity arose I didn't even have the courage to speak to them. They would sit or stand there on the bank, never catching anything or doing anything, yet I found their stillness and

seeming alertness quite impressive. It was extraordinary that grown-ups could appear so purposeful and yet remain so quiescent. Perhaps, if I'd had more time to hang around, I would've seen someone reel in one of the little sardine sized fish that often flickered over the shallows: that would've been exciting–but of course, now I was a schoolboy, I had learned how to be impatient. Also, there were suddenly too many other things to think about, things which my friends insisted I familiarise myself with–like the names of every cowboy who had ever appeared in a comic or on television, from the Cisco Kid to the Range Rider. We also had to learn the vocabulary of Dan Dare, interplanetary space man, as well as Robin Hood and Captain Nemo. Not only did we associate ourselves with these characters, we were them. Once the Indian wars had broken out on the heath, usually after school or at weekends, the pond became almost an irrelevance. We might sometimes have galloped round it, but the fighting was so intense there was no time to stop and stare or even give our horses a drink.

When the wars were over we established a space station in the hollows where Dennis had seen the goblin, but almost as soon as interplanetary flights began we realised that the goblin must, in fact, have been a Martian and consequently things became quite sinister, no one daring to approach the space station on their own. We cancelled all package holiday trips to Mars and would only enter its orbit in the Battle Rocket.

During this crisis I was obviously unable to visit the pond, nor did I think about it, but all the while it was lapping innocently at its grassy banks and the unidentified creatures were truffling contentedly in its ooze.

The great enigma was finally resolved during the blissful freedom of my first summer holidays, when I was walking again round the pond, not alone nor with my spacemen friends, but with my father. He was not as amazed as me to discover an old fisherman who appeared to have actually caught something, and, unlike me, father had no hesitation in going quietly up to him and asking him about it. The angler was sitting on a creel, smoking a pipe and watching his float: at his feet was a long tubular net, with wire hoops, extending into the water, and something inside it was stirring. Responding to father's request, the old chap kindly drew in the net until a miraculous fish was half out of the water, wallowing on its side, looking as fabulous as when I first saw it—or one exactly like it—all that mythical time ago. Close to it seemed terrifyingly huge and strikingly beautiful—its flank evenly covered with large iridescent gold scales, its shape perfectly symmetrical, its fins and tail broad yet fine, almost delicate. It was, said the angler, a carp, and because it had been properly confirmed—almost touched—it was now safe from all those things, like school and alien invasion, that could have destroyed it. Carp: the most sublime example of life on earth that I had ever seen. I wasn't going to be a spaceman any longer. ❧

This is an extract from How To Fish *by Chris Yates, to be published by Hamish Hamilton, November 2006*

WHEN THE WARS WERE OVER WE ESTABLISHED A SPACE STATION IN THE HOLLOWS

Cheers of a Clown

STEPHEN ARMSTRONG **RUNS AWAY AND JOINS THE CIRCUS. PICTURES FROM** 1000 CLOWNS (TASCHEN)

"What is a clown? I will say what they say in Russia. There is one string between universal chaos and our planet. The clown is the person who can pull the string, turn the universe upside down and show people there is another way to live, another magic reality."

Anton Adassinski—founder of Russian clown troupe Derevo

Shangri-La is in the kingdom of Bhutan. Bordering India and China, it's a land of forests, snow-capped mountains, gurgling rivers, whitewashed Buddhist temples and fertile valleys. Local people dress in traditional clothes, tourist numbers are limited and houses, wherever possible, are built from biodegradable materials. It sounds like a happy place. And if you want to know how happy, it's easy to check. Last year, Bhutan started measuring Gross National Happiness and publishing it alongside GDP as a measure of the country's success. In Bhutan, you can tell exactly how happy you are on an annual basis.

Unlike GDP, this happiness measurement isn't published in a single, rigidly definable number (if you're interested, the 60 pages reporting last years GNH can found at www.bhutanstudies.org). What's interesting about the idea, however, is that it's the first time the happiness of a country's citizens has become a matter of public policy. For all Bhutan's isolation, however, it seems to have struck a chord.

This summer, the government announced it was planning a map of the UK based on the happiness of our citizens by 2010. In November, BBC2 showed a four part series called *Making Slough Happy* in which a team of psychologists tried to cheer up the inhabitants of the Thames Valley town. In January, Lord Richard Layard, founder of the Centre for Economic Performance at the London School of Economics, published a paperback version of his book *Happiness*, in which he argues that conventional economics have let us down. According to Layard, the world has assumed that the richer people are, the happier they are, so considers GDP to be a reasonable measure of our joy. He feels this is muddled thinking.

ON A DAMP THURSDAY IN AUGUST I DECIDED TO BECOME A CLOWN

"Levels of happiness in the UK haven't increased since the 1950s," he explains. "We may have more food, more clothes, more cars, bigger houses, more central heating, more holidays, a shorter working week, nicer work and better health, but we are no happier than Britons of fifty years ago. Indeed, all the indicators are that we're actually on a downward slope."

Recently the World Health Organisation announced that clinical depression will become the number one cause of disease and disability over the next ten years. Right now, one in nine Britons show symptoms of depression with one in twenty of us actually clinically depressed. This isn't good, unless you're a poet—in which case, of course, it's a lucrative career opportunity.

For the less inspired, however, being unhappy is bad for you—and not just for those who take their own lives. Psychologists looking back at a project conducted by the mother superior at the American School Sister of Notre Dame in 1932 found some startling evidence of this. She asked all new nuns to write an autobiographical sketch of their life to date, describing how they felt about things as honestly as possible. Some sixty years later, the psychologists rated each story by the amount of positive feeling in the tale then compared that number with the nun's life span. They discovered that the amount of positive vibes the nun was feeling was a pretty good indicator of how long she would live—of the nuns who were still alive in 1991, over half of the least cheerful went on to die in the next nine years whilst less than a quarter of the most cheerful did.

One nun, for instance, wrote "God started my life off well by bestowing upon me inestimable grace. The past year has been a very happy one." She lived to 98. Another ended her account in a more prosaic manner: "With God's grace, I intend to do my best for our Order." She died after a stroke at 59. At a less saintly level, since the Academy Awards began, 750 actors have been nominated for Oscars. Those who won went on to live, on average, four years longer than the losers. When any person has a happy experience, their blood pressure and heart rate falls. Happy people have more robust immune systems and lower levels of stress hormones. If artificially exposed to the flu virus, they are less likely to contract the disease. They are also more likely to recover from major surgery. Clearly getting happy can extend and improve your life. I, however, am a miserable bastard. How can I get happy?

"A clown is like aspirin, only he works twice as fast," *Groucho Marx*

SO IT WAS on a damp Thursday in August I decided to become a clown. It was, I felt sure, the noblest ambition I had yet nursed. The clown is one of the few figures in the cultural world to retain some level of unsettling mystique. Two-bit actors might get caught with their pants down, hard man musicians might take the *Big Brother* shilling, suffering writers might appear on panel shows and blank eyed models might suddenly pontificate on world affairs but the clown remains aloof–hidden behind the grease paint, shrouded in legend and mystery. Be honest, how many other performers can boast a medically recognized phobia like Coulrophobia?

Clowns fascinate. Is it true that each clown's face is as individual as a fingerprint, stored on eggshells in some echoing museum of tomfoolery? Why do their drooping mouths and sparkling eyes switch so effortlessly between the jovial and the terrifying? And after all, my favourite Steinbeck quote showed what an advancement it would be–writers, he said, are a little below clowns and a little above trained seals.

The Academy Of Circus Skills is run by Zippo's Circus as a proper touring circus. It has all the requisite accoutrements–a big top and lorry trailers stacked with tiny double berthed cabins that act as dog kennel homes for the full troupe to live and travel in. It teaches and tours throughout the summer months, with students signing on from May to October. A slight majority of the fledglings are twentysomethings embarking on life's rich journey but there are a very significant number of rat race runaways–accountants who have chucked the actuarial tables in the bin and fled to join the circus. This is not quite the Foreign Legion, but there are plenty of secrets buried beneath the sawdust. It's not considered polite to ask for surnames, for instance. Just in case.

"I see myself as an intelligent, sensitive human, with the soul of a clown which forces me to blow it at the most important moments," *Jim Morrison*

I ARRIVED, PACK IN HAND, at the Henley On Thames leg of last year's season–staggering at dawn into a muddy field belonging to the cute riverside market town's amateur rugby side. At first sight, it didn't bode well. The muddy, churned grass was dotted with caravans and trailers and a stripped big top lay flat on the ground like a flaccid balloon at the end of a four-year-old's party.

I approached cautiously. For one thing, I wasn't sure how carnie folk lived. Were they like actors, drinking and screwing on the adrenalin of every show then staggering out of bed at lunchtime? Or were they as disciplined as dancers, with classes every morning and a rigid schedule dividing up the day? I had assumed the latter. After all, circus folk have a reputation akin to the dark side of faerie. Medieval peasants would cower in their rude shacks as the leering performers cavorted into town, afraid of their glamour (a word coined to describe frozen fascination at an unearthly, magicked beauty) and of their power to bewitch young and impressionable teenagers into throwing away that lucrative potato farm apprenticeship for a life on the open road. She's off with the raggle taggle gypsies oh.

Certainly when I'd visited the vast Montreal based corporate headquarters of the multinational circus corporation that Cirque de Soleil has become, the founder–Guy Laliberte–told me there was something about circus folk that defied his million dollar empire's attempt to normalize them. Even in their Vegas suites, he felt, they would probably sleep on the floor like Mick Dundee. So I practically tiptoed across the Henley ooze, worried that my squelching would infuriate some dozing muscleman or bearded lady and bring wild eyed freaks rushing from their beds crying gabba gabba, we are not like you. And then I met Greg.

> "The artist, like the idiot, or clown, sits on the edge of the world,
> and a push may send him over it," *Osbert Sitwell*

GREG STEPPED OUT OF HIS CARAVAN and seemed, at first sight, depressingly normal. He spoke with a slight New York drawl and was clearly used to giving orders. He was friendly and chatty but there was something hard at the core. "The first thing you can do," he said, "is help us put the top up." And as we hauled on ropes and dropped steel on my feet, he briefed me.

Clowns, it transpires, don't just fling pies and fall over. They have to have a smattering of every circus skill. The fine artists of circus might have honed their rope walking, trapeze or fire eating skills to a level of special forces precision, but the clown is the hardworking footsoldier. Like the infantry, the clown should be able to operate everything proficiently

I would have to learn how to juggle, plate spin, use the trapeze, the unicycle and master a series of prescribed skits like the good/bad routine–an old US vaudeville sketch adapted for clowns in the 30s and 40s. It doesn't play that often to a UK audience, but it's good for getting your timing right.

In "that's good/that's bad", the first clown narrates the gag, the second responds alternately with "that's good /that's bad":

"I found a dog... "

"... that's good."(non-committally)

"It wasn't a hot dog though... " (showing the dog)

"... that's too bad." (looking at the dog, wistfully)

CLOWNS PREFER MONKEY WRENCHES TO SPANNERS, DOOHICKEYS TO GADGETS AND WOULD MUCH PREFER TO BE FIDGETY THAN RESTLESS

"He's really friendly..."

"Oh, that's good... "

"... with people's legs."

—"Well *that's* bad."

"He doesn't eat much..."

"... that's good."

"He sure poops a lot though... "

"... that's bad."

"He's housebroken... "

"... that's good!"

"No, that's bad, he did some jail time for the last housebreak."

"OK, then that's bad..."

"No, that's good—it was his second offence. He's gone straight now... "

"That's... uhhh... good?"

"No, that's bad, he's gone straight for your pastrami sandwich!"

Pastrami is better than corned beef because pastrami is funny and corned beef isn't. Likewise— clowns prefer monkey wrenches to spanners, doohickeys to gadgets and would much prefer to be fidgety than restless. And then I started paying in sweat.

Juggling proved way more complicated that I'd thought given the number of idiots chucking balls about as street performers. I'd figured that if crusties can do it, it can't be hard. Astonishingly, it was. Perhaps that's why they don't have time to bath. Juggling didn't feel like fun—it felt like chucking balls about badly. Once onto plate spinning, however, the real clowning came in. In a surprisingly short time, I was whisking plates on a pole and—for a cak handed beanpole like me—it was a joyous business. You couldn't take the grin off my face.

Trapeze was a matter of courage rather than skill. Hanging upside down on a rope is just about having the gumption to hurl your body when required and damn the consequences. And then the full clown make-up was on and I was slap sticking through a quick routine with Greg. He'd seen me as Auguste—an auburn faced clown whose role is to have his pompous self importance knocked out of him and encourage the audience to warm to the downtrodden hero clown. Behind the mask of the paint, I did things I hadn't done since the playground. I mugged. I cackled. I threw myself about the ring. In short, I genuinely felt like a kid again. Something about the make up and the pratfalls took away my uptight hardworking careworn expression and made me into an absolute gleeful idiot.

And so I propose a clown revolution. After all, if, when Lenin said "freedom is so important it has to be rationed," he'd been wearing a fluffy wig and big red nose no-one would have taken him seriously. Who can possibly argue that society would not be better if people honked when you pinched their noses, if cars fell apart after only 20 feet and if the slime and detritus of everyday living could be turned into confetti simply by putting it in a bucket and throwing it at people. There's even a revolutionary clown manifesto, forged by US agitators at Clownarchy.org. It includes the following clauses:

We hereby decree that henceforth and effective immediately
we shall heed to no decrees.

...

We will speak the truth with humour. Verily I say, even the
mimes among us shall not be silenced.

...

Our noses are red from the having drunk too much of the intoxicant we call
"society". Recognising that we are powerless over this intoxicant is the first
step. (There are 11 other steps too!)

...

Our minds will not be controlled by the backwards logic of others,
but rather by our own backwards logic.

Clowns hold a very important role in many cultures around the world. In becoming a clown I realise that I truly have some big shoes to fill.

But perhaps the last word goes to the greatest clown of all, the South London lad who took on Hitler, stood up to McCarthy and did so whilst hardly saying a word:

"I remain just one thing, and one thing only—and that is a clown. It places me on
a far higher plane than any politician," *Charlie Chaplin* ◉

All images taken from the fantastic 1000 Clowns *by H Thomas Steele, published by Taschen.*
Zippo's Academy runs six-month training programmes with no age limits. For those keen to run
away and joining the circus, tel: 07050 28 26 24

Poet of Indolence

NICHOLAS LEZARD ON HOW SAMUEL BECKETT
PULLED HIM OUT OF THE WORKADAY WORLD.
PHOTOGRAPH BY JOHN MINIHAN

The editor of this very magazine recently presented me with a copy of his book, *How to be Idle.* "To Nick," he inscribed it, "who showed me the way." Generous, that, and touching. Not, incidentally, that he has taken the way I showed him: for, after all, he has written a book, and works like Stakhanov to produce the magazine you hold in your hands. The true testimony to idleness can never be written; for writing of any worth is effortful, as I am sure Tom knows by now.

So, if we may say that in a lifetime of non-achievement, of neglecting any small talent I have lest it tempt me to fortune and recognition, I have written the book of idleness by, precisely, not writing it, who, you might ask, showed ME the way? Who made me so idle that I barely have the energy to denounce, tongue half in cheek, the editor of the *Idler*?

Step forward, if he can be arsed, one Samuel Barclay Beckett, born one hundred years ago in April, in Dublin, winner of the Nobel Prize for Literature, number eight batsman and economical bowler for Trinity College, Dublin; taciturn resistance hero, sufferer from countless psychosomatic diseases, man of limitless integrity, lecturer at the Ecole Normale Superieure, the cleverest place in the world, dangerous driver, lover of drink and tobacco and prostitutes, amanuensis and proselytiser of James Joyce, implacable enemy of compromise, master of silence, and author of the most scabrous, exciting, meaningful, hair-raising, unconventional, fearless and hilarious prose of the twentieth century.

I first came across his work, like you probably did or will, with Waiting for Godot. It happened like this. It was the end of the summer holidays. I was about to start studying A-Level English. I had been assigned a large reading list. With more pressing matters to attend to than read—such as, for instance, the necessity of masturbating myself into an appalled stupor by lunchtime (seven times per diem a fairly average figure)—I found myself, ten days before school started again, with a large reading list and not a sentence of it actually read. I went to a bookshop and did some drastic whittling-down on the spot. I found one of the books: *Waiting for Godot*. It was short. That was good. Blindly, I reached for another: *Middlemarch*. It was not short, and that was not good. But its substantiality counted for it, and my future reputation. "At least I've read *Middlemarch*," I would be able to tell myself, and anyone else who cared to listen.

I did, in the end. To ask a barely fifteen-year-old boy to read one hundred pages a day, minimum, of clotted and earnest Victorian prose, and come out with any other feeling than resentment, is to ask too much. So when I turned to *Godot*, even the physical sensation of lifting up this wafer-thin book was like being relieved of a heavy burden. Reading it, I felt positively exalted. In place of the tangled who-gives-a-fuck web of frustration and thwarted love in the boondocks (the only remotely sympathetic character in *Middlemarch*, I grumpily thought, was Casaubon; as I was about to discover, this was because he was the most Beckettian), here was a stage direction consisting of three mercifully short sentences: "A country road. A tree. Evening."

There then followed the non-adventures of two shabby gentlemen who had a fantastically indolent attitude to life. And then, as the evidence of my morning's self-pollution encrusted about me (see paragraph 4 above), I came across, so to speak, the following exchange:

[Silence. ESTRAGON looks attentively at the tree.]
VLADIMIR: What do we do now?
ESTRAGON: Wait.
VLADIMIR: Yes, but while waiting.
ESTRAGON: What about hanging ourselves?
VLADIMIR: Hmm. It'd give us an erection!
ESTRAGON: [Highly excited.] An erection!

Well, that was it for me. Although at a pinch you could argue that even *Middlemarch* is better wanking material than anything in Beckett, this at least spoke to me. It is not the size of the book that matters if you want to have your horizons expanded.

There is no need here to dwell on *Godot*. Or too much on the next play of his that I read, and he wrote, *Endgame*, except to quote one of the finest considered blasphemies ever to have been written by humanity. After a brief period of attempted prayer to

God, during which no-one hears anything but silence, we are treated to the line: "The bastard! He doesn't exist!" This got Beckett into a bit of a scrape with the Lord Chancellor, who at the time had ultimate authority over the content of any publicly-performed play in the country. But it was fine by me.

After that, and with the help of a sympathetic, if perhaps somewhat concerned English teacher, I was off to the library to find everything the man had written. At the time, remember, I was a frustrated (see paragraph 4 above) and disturbed adolescent; I was disgruntled with the world, having noticed that it was not all it was cracked up to be. I was listening to an awful lot of Joy Division. Now, not all Beckett's work is funny, I had better warn you. The world, as he put it most pithily in his novel *Watt*, is "an excrement". And while this can be funny some of the time, it is not so all of the time, not at least if you are going to stare it full in the face and take its measure. Laughter is a response, a necessary response, but it is not the only response, and for every big yok there are several groans of despair. And Joy Division, who never really had a sunny side to them, went with the bleak Beckettian worldview like tea and biscuits. When I had sated my contempt for the universe with text, I would turn to the sparsely-produced, angular soundworld of Joy Division, existential Mancunian despair made audible, and top myself up musically. And when I had done that, refreshed, off I would go to Beckett. Did I ever really have a hope?

And then I went to Paris. I had saved up enough money to starve myself in a chambre de bonne for three months before going to university. I had a room about the size of a speaker cabinet, a sink the size of a specimen jar, no phone, one friend a two-mile walk away, and a load of books. Guess who some of them were by. I also had Deirdre Bair's biography of Beckett, and from that indiscreet document I deduced the location of his

JOY DIVISION, WHO NEVER REALLY HAD A SUNNY SIDE TO THEM, WENT WITH THE BLEAK BECKETTIAN WORLDVIEW LIKE TEA AND BISCUITS.

THIS WAS A MAN
WHO VALUED NOT
ONLY HIS SILENCE,
BUT ALL SILENCE.

flat—a hop and a shuffle on the metro from where I festered.

I lurked outside his front door for a while. I could see his name on a mailbox in the hall. All I had to do was wait long enough—how hard could that be?—and he would emerge, I would clasp his hand, and we would be Friends.

A moment's reflection, and a quick re-read of the oeuvre, and I realised how much of an affront that would be. For this was a man who valued not only his silence, but all silence. He was no friendless freak, for all that so many of his characters are, but only the most insensitive clod could imagine that he would be delighted if a stranger came bounding up to him like a randy dog (of which there, incidentally, one or two in Beckett's work).

So I retreated back to the work, and let him be. (Since then I have met any number of people who were not so shy, and who regaled me with their tales of how they walked the streets of Paris silently together, or got him to agree to be the Honorary President of their cricket team. I wish them all blasted to hell.) And there is plenty to be getting on with in the work. Or, to put it another way, plenty to be getting on with, or plenty of nothing to be getting on with. Beckett is not one for believing that if a job is worth doing, it is worth doing well. No job is worth doing. Take his hero, Murphy, and his rant at his girlfriend, who, although decent enough in her way, keeps trying to get him to get a job:

"Ever since June," he said, "it has been job, job, job, nothing but job. Nothing happens in the world but is specially designed to exalt me into a job. I say a job is the end of us both, or at least of me. You say no, but the beginning. I am to be a new man, you are to be a new woman, the entire sublunary excrement will turn to civet, there will be more joy in heaven over Murphy finding a job than over the billions of leatherbums that never had anything else."

But life, of course, is bad enough without a job. It is not enough to curse the day of your birth. In his masterful radio play—how many opportunities do you ever get to say that? But he wrote beautifully for the medium, like no other playwright—a Mr Tyler is asked what he is doing. "Nothing, Mrs Rooney, nothing. I was merely cursing, under my breath, God and man, under my breath, and the wet Saturday afternoon of my conception." Even venery is no release. This, from *First Love*:

> "You disturb me, I said, I can't stretch out with you there. The collar of my greatcoat was over my mouth and yet she heard me. Must you stretch out? She said. The mistake one makes is to speak to people. You only have to put your feet on my knees, she said. I didn't wait to be asked twice, under my miserable calves I felt her fat thighs. She began stroking my ankles. I considered kicking her in the cunt."

At which point the more sensitive may recoil. At which you must say patiently that Beckett does not advocate kicking anyone in the cunt, this is a character he created who is contemplating it. It is not about kicking people in the cunt, it is about jerking us out of our complacencies.

Literature worth the name, you may be surprised to hear, comes with responsibilities, which may be summed up like this: if you are unfortunate enough to know someone with far too much money, for example, and you see anything by, say, Orwell or Dickens on their shelves, then you have the duty to ask: Excuse me, have you actually read this? And were you paying attention? The second question, if you'd asked it in Latin, would have taken the interrogative form in which the answer "no" is expected. You then have the right and duty to confiscate the relevant volume(s). Similarly if you see anything by Beckett in the possession of a plutocrat, or someone in management, or anyone with who is unjustifiably content with the world and their place in it. For Beckett is the sworn enemy of the happy camper. His only happy campers exist in his first novel, Murphy, and they are found in an asylum for the insane. Murphy, although not exactly Beckett, is odd enough for him to have only come from Beckett's mind; a projection of it, if you will. And when Murphy, whose antipathy for employment should be saluted by everyone who has secured a copy of this magazine, finally gives in to his girlfriend's demands that he get a job, finally meets his charges, "They caused Murphy no horror. The most easily identifiable of his immediate feelings were respect and unworthiness. Except for the manic, who was like an epitome of all the self-made plutolaters who ever triumphed over empty pockets and clean hands, the impression he received was of that self-immersed indifference to the contingencies of the contingent world which he had chosen for himself as the only felicity and achieved so seldom."

And that, ladies and gentlemen, is how you achieve felicity. You just pull yourself out of the workaday world. Beckett will show you how. ◉

Freedom versus Authority in Education

IN THIS WISE 1928 ESSAY, BERTRAND RUSSELL ADVOCATES A LOT OF FREEDOM FOR KIDS, AND THE MINIMUM OF AUTHORITY. ILLUSTRATIONS BY NICKY DEELEY

Freedom, in education as in other things, must be a matter of degree. Some freedoms cannot be tolerated. I met a lady once who maintained that no child should ever be forbidden to do anything, because a child ought to develop its nature from within. "How if its nature leads it to swallow pins?" I asked; but I regret to say the answer was mere vituperation. And yet every child, left to itself, will sooner or later swallow pins, or drink poison out of medicine bottles, or fall out of an upper window, or otherwise bring itself to a bad end. At a slightly later age, boys, when they have the opportunity, will go unwashed, overeat, smoke till they are sick, catch chills from sitting in wet feet, and so on—let alone the fact that they will amuse themselves by plaguing elderly gentlemen, who may not all have Elisha's powers of repartee. Therefore one who advocates freedom in education cannot mean that children should do exactly as they please all day long. An element of discipline and authority must exist; the question is as to the amount of it, and the way in which it is to be exercised.

Education may be viewed from many standpoints: that of the State, of the Church, of the schoolmaster, of the parents, or even (though this is usually forgotten) of the child itself. Each of these points of view is partial; each contributes elements that are bad. Let us examine them successively, and see what is to be said for and against them.

W e will begin with the State, as the most powerful force in deciding what modern education is to be. The interest of the State in education is very recent. It did not exist in antiquity or the Middle Ages; until the Renaissance, education was only valued by the Church. The Renaissance brought an interest in advanced scholarship, leading to the foundation of such institutions as the Collège de France, intended to offset the ecclesiastical Sorbonne. The Reformation, in England and Germany, brought a desire on the part of the State to have some control over universities and grammar schools, to prevent them from remaining hotbeds of "Popery". But this interest soon evaporated. The State took no decisive or continuous part until the quite modern movement for universal compulsory education. Nevertheless the State, now, has more to say to scholastic institutions than have all the other factors combined.

The motives which led to universal compulsory education were various. Its strongest advocates were moved by the feeling that it is in itself desirable to be able to read and write, that an ignorant population is a disgrace to a civilised country, and that democracy is impossible without education. These motives were reinforced by others. It was soon seen that education gave commercial advantages, that it diminished juvenile crime, and that it gave opportunities for regimenting slum populations. Anti-clericals perceived in State education an opportunity of combating the influence of the Church; this motive weighed considerably in England and France. Nationalists, especially after the Franco-Prussian War, considered that universal education would increase the national strength. All these reasons, however, were at first subsidiary. The main reason for adopting universal education was the feeling that illiteracy was disgraceful.

This institution, once firmly established, was found by the State to be capable of many uses. It makes young people more docile, both for good and evil. It improves manners and diminishes crime; it facilitates common action for public ends; it makes the community more responsive to direction from a centre. Without it, democracy cannot exist except as an empty form. But democracy, as conceived by politicians, is a form of government, that is to say, it is a method of making people do what their leaders wish under the impression that they are doing what they themselves wish. Accordingly, State education has acquired a certain bias. It teaches the young (so far as it can) to respect existing institutions, to avoid all fundamental criticism of the powers that be, and to regard foreign nations with suspicion and contempt. It increases national solidarity at the expense both of internationalism and of individual development. The damage to individual development comes though the undue stress upon authority. Collective rather than individual emotions are encouraged and disagreement with prevailing beliefs is severely repressed. Uniformity is desired because it is convenient to the administrator, regardless of the fact that it can only be secured by mental atrophy. So great are the resulting evils that it can be seriously questioned whether universal education has hitherto done good or harm on the balance.

The point of view of the Church as regards education is, in practice, not very different from that of the State. There is, however, one important divergence: the Church would prefer that the laity should not be educated at all, and only give them instruction when the State insists. The State and the Church both wish to instil beliefs which are likely to be dispelled by free enquiry. But the State creed is easier to instil into a population which can read a newspaper, whereas the Church creed is easier to instil into a wholly illiterate population. State and Church are both hostile to instruction. This will pass, and is passing, as the ecclesiastical authorities perfect the technique of giving instruction without stimulating mental activity—a technique in which, long ago, the Jesuits led the way.

The schoolmaster, in the modern world, is seldom allowed a point of view of his own. He is appointed by an education authority and is "sacked" if he is found to be educating. Apart from this economic motive, the schoolmaster is exposed to temptations of which he is likely to be unconscious. He stands, even more directly than the State and the Church, for discipline; officially he knows what his pupils do not know. Without some element of discipline and authority, it is difficult to keep a class in order. It is easier to punish a boy for showing boredom than it is to be interesting. Moreover, even the best schoolmaster is likely to exaggerate his importance, and to deem it possible and desirable to mould his pupils into the sort of human beings that he thinks they ought to be. Lytton Strachey describes Dr Arnold

IT IS EASIER TO
PUNISH A BOY FOR
SHOWING BOREDOM
THAN IT IS TO BE
INTERESTING

walking beside the lake of Como and meditating on "moral evil". Moral evil, for him, was whatever he wished to change in his boys. The belief that there was a great deal of it in them justified him in the exercise of power, and in conceiving of himself as a ruler whose duty was even more to chasten than to love. This attitude—variously phrased in various ages—is natural to any schoolmaster who is zealous without being on the watch for the deceitful influence of self-importance. Nevertheless the teacher is far the best of the forces concerned in education, and it primarily to him or her that we must look for progress.

Then again the schoolmaster wants the credit of his school. This makes him wish to have his boys distinguish themselves in athletic contests and scholarship examinations, which leads to care for a certain selection of superior boys to the exclusion of others. For the rank and file, the result is bad. It is much better for a boy to play a game badly himself than to watch others playing it well. Mr HG Wells, in his *Life of Sanderson of Oundle*, tells how this really great schoolmaster set his face against everything that left the faculties of the average boy unexercised and uncared-for. When he became headmaster, he found that only certain selected boys were expected to sing in chapel; they were trained as a choir, and the rest listened. Sanderson insisted that all should sing, whether musical or not. In this he was rising above the bias which is natural to a schoolmaster who cares more for his credit than for his boys. Of course, if we all apportioned credit wisely there would be no conflict between these two motives: the school which did best by the boys would get the most credit. But in a busy world spectacular successes will always win credit out of proportion to their real importance. So that some conflict between the two motives is hardly avoidable.

I come now to the point of view of the parent. This differs according to the economic status of the parent: the average wage-earner has desires quite different from those of the average professional man. The average wage-earner wishes to get his children to school as soon as possible, so as to diminish bother at home; he also wishes to get them away as soon as possible, so as to profit by their earnings. When recently the British Government decided to cut down expenditure on education, it proposed that children should not go to school before the age of six, and should not be obliged to stay after the age of thirteen. The former proposal caused such a popular outcry that it had to be dropped: the indignation of worried mothers (recently enfranchised) was irresistible. The latter proposal, lowering the age for leaving school, was not unpopular. Parliamentary candidates advocating better education would get unanimous applause from those who came to meetings, but would find, in canvassing, that unpolitical wage-earners (who are the majority) want their chidren to be free to get paid work as soon as possible. The exceptions are mainly those who hope that their children may rise in the social scale through better education.

Professional men have quite a different outlook. Their own income depends upon the fact that they have had a better education than the average, and they wish to hand on this advantage to their children. For this object they are willing to make great sacrifices. But in our present competitive society, what will be desired by the average parent is not an education which is good in itself, but an education which is better than other people's. This may be facilitated by keeping down the general level, and

NEITHER HAPPINESS OR VIRTUE, BUT WORLDY SUCCESS, IS WHAT THE AVERAGE FATHER DESIRES FOR HIS CHILDREN

therefore we cannot expect a professional man to be enthusiastic about facilities for higher education for the children of wage-earners. If everybody who desired it could get a medical education, however poor his parents might be, it is obvious that doctors would earn less than they do, both from increased competition and from the improved health of the community. The same thing applies to the law, the civil service, and so on. Thus the good things which the professional man desires for his own children he will not desire for the bulk of the population unless he has exceptional public spirit.

The fundamental defect of fathers, in our competitive society, is that they want their children to be a credit to them. This is rooted in instinct, and can only be cured by efforts directed to that end. The defect exists also, though to a lesser degree, in mothers. We all feel instinctively, that our children's successes reflect glory upon ourselves, while their failures make us feel shame. Unfortunately, the successes which cause us to swell with pride are often of an undesirable kind. From the dawn of civilisation till almost our own time–and still in China and Japan–parents have sacrificed their children's happiness in marriage by deciding whom they were to marry, choosing almost always the richest bride or bridegroom available. In the Western world (except partially in France) children have freed themselves from this slavery by rebellion, but parents' instincts have not changed. Neither happiness or virtue, but worldly success, is what the average father desires for his children. He wants them to be such as he can boast to his cronies, and this desire largely dominates his efforts for their education.

Authority, if it is to govern education, must rest upon one or several of the powers we have considered: the State, the Church, the schoolmaster and the parent. We have seen that not one of them can be trusted to care adequately for the child's welfare, since each wishes the child to minister to some end which has nothing to do with his own well-being. The State wants the child to serve for national aggrandisement and the support of existing forms of government. The Church wants the child to serve for increasing the power of the priesthood. The schoolmaster, in a competitive world, too often regards his school as the State regards the nation, and the parent wants the child to glorify the family. The child itself, as an end in itself, as a separate human being with a claim to whatever happiness and well-being may be possible, does not come into these various external purposes, except very partially. Unfortunately, the child lacks the experience required for the guidance of its own life, and is therefore a prey to the sinister interests that batten on its innocence. This is what makes the difficulty of education as a political problem. But let us first see what can be said from the child's point of view.

It is obvious that most children, if they were left to themselves, would not learn to read and write, and would grow up less adapted than they might be to the circumstances of their lives. There must be educational institutions, and the children must be to some extent under authority. But in view of the fact no authority can be wholly trusted, we must aim at having as little authority as possible, and try to think out ways by which young people's natural desires and impulses can be utilised in education. This is far more possible than is often thought, for, after all, the desire to acquire knowledge is natural to most young people. The traditional pedagogue, possessing knowledge not worth imparting, and devoid of all skill in imparting it, imagined that young people had a native horror of instruction, but in this he was misled by failure to realise his own shortcomings. There is a charming tale of Chekov's about a man who tried to teach a kitten to catch mice. When it wouldn't run after them, he beat it, with the result that even as an adult cat, it cowered with terror in the presence of a mouse. "This is the man," Chekov adds, "who taught me Latin." Now cats teach their kitten to catch mice, but they wait till the instinct has awakened. Then the kittens agree with their mammas that the knowledge is worth acquiring, so that discipline is not required.

The first two or three years of life have hitherto escaped the domination of the pedagogue, and all authorities are agreed that those are the years in which we learn most. Every child learns to talk by its own efforts. Anyone who has watched an infant knows that the efforts required are very considerable. The child listens intently, watches movements of the lips, practises sounds all day long, and concentrates with amazing ardour. Of course grown-up people encourage it by praise, but it does not occur to them to punish it on days when it learns no new word. All that they provide is opportunity and praise. It is doubtful whether more is required at any stage.

What is necessary is to make the child or young person feel that the knowledge is worth having. Sometimes this is difficult because in fact the knowledge is not worth having. It is also difficult when only a considerable amount of knowledge in any direction is useful, so that at first the pupil tends to be merely bored. In such cases, however, the difficulty is not insuperable. Take, for instance, the teaching of mathematics. Sanderson of Oundle found that almost all his boys were interested in machinery, and he provided them with opportunities for making quite elaborate machines. In the course of this practical work, they came upon the necessity for making calculations, and thus grew interested in mathematics as required for the success of a constructive enterprise on which they were keen. This method is expensive, and involves patient skill on the part of the teacher. But it goes along the lines of the pupil's instinct, and is therefore likely to involve less boredom with more intellectual effort. Effort is natural both to animals and men, but it must be effort for which there is an instinctive stimulus. A football match involves more effort than the treadmill, yet the one is a pleasure and the other a punishment. It is a mistake to suppose that mental effort can rarely be a pleasure; what is true is that certain conditions are required to make it pleasurable, and that, until lately, no attempt was made to create those conditions in education. The chief conditions are: first, a problem of which the solution is desired; secondly, a feeling of hopefulness as to the possibility of obtaining a solution. Consider the way David Copperfield was taught Arithmetic:

> Even when the lessons are done, the worst is yet to happen, in the shape of an appalling sum. This is invented for me, and delivered to me orally by Mr Murdstone, and begins, "If I go into a cheesemonger's shop, and buy five thousand double-Gloucester cheeses at fourpence-halfpenny each, present payment"—at which I see Mr Murdstone secretly overjoyed. I pore over the cheeses without any result or enlightenment until dinner-time; when, having made a mulatto of myself by getting the dirt of the slate into the pores of my skin, I have a slice of bread to help me out with the cheeses, and am considered in disgrace for the rest of the evening.

Obviously the poor boy could not be expected to take any interest in the cheeses, or to have any hope of doing the sum right. If he had wanted a box of a certain size, and had been told to save up his allowance until he could buy enough wood and nails, it would have stimulated his arithmetical powers amazingly.

[...]

I do not maintain that all children can have their intellectual interests aroused by suitable stimuli. Some have much less than average intelligence, and require special treatment. It is very undesirable to combine in one class children whose mental capacities are very different: the cleverer ones will be bored by having things explained that they clearly understand, and the stupider ones will be worried by having things taken for granted that they have not yet grasped. But subjects and methods should be adapted to the intelligence of the pupil. Macaulay was made to learn mathematics at Cambridge, but it is obvious from his letters that it was a sheer waste of time. I was made to learn Latin and Greek, but I resented it, being of the opinion that it was silly to learn a language that was no longer spoken. I believe that all the little good I got from years of classical studies I could have got in adult life in a month. After the bare minimum, account should be taken of tastes, and pupils should only be taught what they find interesting. This puts a strain upon teachers, who find it easier to be dull, especially if they are over-worked. But the difficulties can be overcome by giving teachers shorter hours and instruction in the art of teaching, which is done at present in training teachers in elementary schools, but not teachers in universities or public schools.

Freedom in education has many aspects. There is first of all freedom to learn or not to learn. Then there is freedom as to what to learn. And in late education there is freedom of opinion. Freedom to learn or not to learn can be only partially conceded in childhood. It is necessary to make sure that all who are not imbecilic learn to read and write. How far this can be done by the mere provision of opportunity, only experience can show. But even if opportunity alone suffices, children must have the opportunity thrust upon them. Most of them would rather play outdoors, where the necessary opportunities would be lacking. Later on, it might be left to the choice of young people whether, for instance, they should go to the university; some would wish to do so, others would not. This would make quite as good a principle of selection as any to be got from entrance examinations. Nobody who did not work should be allowed to stay at the university. The rich young men who now waste their time in college are demoralising others and teaching themselves to be useless. If hard work were exacted as a condition of residence, universities would cease to be attractive to people with a distaste for intellectual pursuits.

Freedom as to what to learn ought to exist far more than at present. I think it is necessary to group subjects by their natural affinities; there are grave disadvantages in the elective system, which leaves a young man free to choose wholly unconnected subjects. If I were organising education in Utopia, with unlimited funds, I should give every child, at the age of about twelve, some instruction in classics, mathematics, and science. After two years, it ought to be evident where the child's aptitudes lay, and the child's own tastes would be a safe indication, provided there were no "soft options". Consequently I should allow every boy and girl who so desired to specialise from the age of fourteen. At first, the specialisation would be very broad, growing gradually more defined as education advanced. The time when it was possible to be universally well-informed is past. An industrious man may know something of history and literature, which requires a knowledge of classical and modern languages. Or he may know some parts of mathematics, or one or two sciences. But the ideal of an "all-round" education is out of date; it has been destroyed by the progress of knowledge.

Freedom of opinion, on the part of both teachers and pupils, is the most important of the various kinds of freedom, and the only one which requires no limitations whatever. In view of the fact that it does not exist, it is worth while to recapitulate the argument in its favour.

The fundamental argument for freedom of opinion is the doubtfulness of all our beliefs. If we certainly knew the truth, there would be something to be said for teaching it. But in that case it could not be taught without invoking authority, by means of its inherent reasonableness. It is not necessary to make a law that no one should be allowed to teach arithmetic if he holds heretical opinions on the multiplication table, because here the truth is clear, and does not require to be forced by penalties. When the State intervenes to ensure the teaching of some doctrine, it does so because there is no conclusive evidence in favour of that doctrine. The result is that teaching is not truthful, even if it should happen to be true. In the State of New York, it was till lately illegal to teach that Communism is good; in Soviet Russia, it is illegal to teach that Communism is bad. No doubt one of these opinions is true and one false, but no one knows which. Either New York or Soviet Russia was teaching truth and proscribing falsehood, but neither was teaching truthfully, because each was representing a doubtful proposition as certain.

The difference between truth and truthfulness is important in this connection. Truth is for the gods; from our point of view, it is an ideal, towards which we can approximate, but which we cannot hope to reach. Education should fit us for the nearest possible approach to truth, and to do this it must teach truthfulness. Truthfulness, as I mean it, is the habit of forming our opinions on the evidence, and holding them with that degree of conviction which the evidence warrants. This degree will always fall short of complete certainty, and therefore we must be always ready to admit new evidence against previous beliefs. Moreover, when we act on a belief, we must, if possible, only take action as will be useful even if our belief is more or less inaccurate; we should avoid actions which are disastrous unless our belief is exactly true. In science, an observer states his results along with the "probable error"; but who ever heard of a theologian or a politician stating the probable error in his dogmas, or even admitting that any error is conceivable? That is because in science, where we approach nearest to real knowledge, a man can safely rely on the strength of his case, whereas, where nothing is known, blatant assertion and hypnotism are the usual ways of causing others to share our beliefs. If the fundamentalists thought they had a good case against evolution, they would not make the teaching of it illegal.

The habit of teaching someone orthodoxy, political, religious, or moral, has all kinds of bad effects. To begin with, it excludes from the teaching profession men likely to have the best moral and mental effect upon their pupils. I will give three illustrations. First, as to politics: a teacher of economics in America is expected to teach such doctrines as will add to the wealth and power of the very rich; if he does not, he finds it advisable to go elsewhere, like Mr Laski, formerly of Harvard, now one of the most valuable teachers in the London School of Economics. Second, as to religion: the immense majority of intellectually eminent men disbelieve the Christian religion, but they conceal the fact in public, because they are afraid of losing their incomes. Thus on the most important of all subjects most of the men whose opinions and arguments would be best worth having are condemned to silence. Third, as to morals: Practically all men are unchaste at some time of their lives; clearly those who conceal this fact are worse than those who do not. Since they add the guilt of hypocrisy. But it is only to the hypocrites that teaching posts are open. So much for the effects of orthodoxy upon the choice and character of teachers.

I come now to the effect upon the pupils, which I will take under two heads, intellectually and moral. Intellectually, what is stimulating to a young man is a problem of obvious practical importance, as to which he finds that divergent opinions are held. A young man learning economics, for example, ought to hear lectures from individualists and socialists, protectionists and free-traders, inflationists and believers in the gold standard. He ought to be encouraged to read the best books of the various schools, as recommended by those who believe in them. This would teach him to weigh arguments and evidence, to know that no opinion is certainly right, and to judge men by their quality rather than by their consonance with preconceptions. History should be taught not only from the point of view of one's own country, but also from that of foreigners. If history were taught by Frenchmen in England, and by Englishmen in France, there would be no disagreements between the two countries, each would understand the other's point of view. A young man should learn to think that all questions are open, and that an argument should be followed wherever it leads. The needs of practical life will destroy this attitude all too soon when he begins to earn his living; but until that time he should be encouraged to taste the joys of free speculation.

Morally, also, the teaching of an orthodoxy to the young is very harmful. There is not only the fact that it compels the abler teachers to be hypocrites, and therefore to set a bad moral example. There is also, what is more important, the fact that it encourages intolerance and the bad forms of herd instinct. Edmund Gosse, in his *Father and Son*, relates how, when he was a boy, his father told him he was going to marry again. The boy saw there was something his father was ashamed of, so at last he asked, in accents or horror: "Father, is she a Paedo-Baptist?" And she was. Until that moment, he had believed all Paedo-Baptists to be wicked. So children in Catholic schools believe that Protestants are wicked, children in any school in an Engish-speaking country believe that atheists are wicked, and children in Germany believe that Frenchmen are wicked. When a school accepts as part of its task the teaching of an opinion which cannot be intellectually defended (as practically all schools do), it is compelled to give the impression that those who hold an opposite opinion are wicked, since otherwise it cannot generate the passion required for repelling the assaults of reason. Thus for the sake of orthodoxy the children are rendered uncharitable, intolerant, cruel, and bellicose. This is unavoidable so long as definite opinions are prescribed on politics, morals, and religion.

Finally, arising out of this moral damage to the individual, there is untold damage to society. Wars and persecutions are rife everywhere, and everywhere they are rendered possible by the teaching in the schools. Wellington used to say that the battle of Waterloo was won on the playing fields of Eton. He might have said with more truth that the war against revolutionary France was instigated in the classrooms of Eton. In our democratic age, Eton has become unimportant; now, it is the ordinary elementary and secondary school that matters. In every country, by means of flag-waving, Empire Day, Fourth-of-July celebrations, Officer's Training Corps, etc., everything is done to give boys a taste for homicide, and girls a conviction that men given to homicide are the most worthy of respect. This whole system of moral degradation to which innocent boys and girls are exposed would become impossible if the authorities allowed freedom of opinion to teachers and pupils.

Regimentation is the source of the evil. Education authorities do not look on children, as religion is supposed to do, as human beings with souls to be saved. They look upon them as material for grandiose social schemes: future "hands" in factories or "bayonets" in war and what not. No man is fit to educate unless he feels each pupil an end in himself with his own rights, and his own personality, not merely a piece in a jig-saw puzzle, or a soldier in a regiment, or a citizen in a State. Reverence for human personality is the beginning of wisdom, in every social question, but above all in education. ❧

STORIES

The Chronicles of Peregrine Beer

IN WHICH BRITAIN'S DRUNKEST BIRDWATCHER PAYS
A VISIT TO HIS BROTHER'S KILBURN FLAT.
STORY AND ILLUSTRATION BY JOCK SCOT

"I'll just have a wee dram first to get my lungs functioning," said Shed. "Would you like a glass of opium tea? I have a small ball from last year's harvest, still retains it's flavour remarkably well."

"Splendid suggestion Shed! That should set us up nicely for some skirling and birling. What a grand host you are!"

Shed scuttled off to prepare the opium tea and fetch his bagpipes, and Perry engaged Pedro in more gay banter.

"My brother never married, yet, as a young man, the beautiful girls, and boys, of London society threw themselves at him. He was charmingly, blissfully unaware of his desirability. He perplexed them all by preferring to potter round in the garden, or bury his head in some wordy tome rather than attend dinner parties and then of course, there was his fascination with psychotropic drugs and mind-expansion. That saw off quite a few, they just couldn't keep up with him. Never mind his dedication to playing the bagpipes, the boy's a virtuoso! Ah! Here he is now, come, give us a tune! I'll pour the tea." Shed passed the tray to his brother and wandered off down to the bottom of the garden where he entered a garden shed, closed the door and began tuning up. Perry poured the tea into half-pint glasses which sat in metal frames with handles. "No milk needed with this brew Pedro, but it does improve the taste if you add sugar. One lump or two?"

They could hear muted bagpipe strains coming from the shed where Shed was tuning up. Shed spent a lot of time in the shed, which was how he got his nickname. His birth-name was Shenandoah, as he had been conceived in an hotel at Harper's Ferry on the banks of the River Shenandoah in Virginia, USA during his parents' honeymoon. When he first ventured into his father's shed he had been taken with the fusty, dusty atmosphere and the otherworldly privacy contained therein. He was about seven years old at the time

"HAS ANYONE EVER TOLD YOU THAT YOU'RE A DEAD RINGER FOR KATE MOSS?" HE CHIRUPPED. "I AM KATE MOSS, YOU SILLY SCOTSMAN!"

and had just begun smoking, so it was the perfect spot to indulge his forbidden habit. When he discovered a large stash of pornography tucked away beneath copies of *Gardeners' World* it became his home-from-home.

He emerged now, satisfied that he was in tune, though the untutored listener may have thought otherwise. He was really letting rip, the long-tailed tits, a robin and a wren flew off to seek sanctuary several gardens away, pursued by a silver tabby cat which had been eyeing them up from a patch of long grass. Shed, his face bright red with effort, cheeks distended like Dizzy Gillespie, trod around the lawn in a most curious fashion. He seemed to be attempting to goose-step, but in slow motion!

Pedro resisted the temptation to stick fingers in his ears, he'd heard a lot worse from support bands, and listened attentively with a fixed grin on his face. You didn't really have to listen, the noise was deafening and could probably be heard over on Portobello Road.

"When shall we head off down to the gig, Pedro? You're on at 9.30," said Perry.

"No. I no go. I think as singer of Libertines tribute band it is good if I no turn up.

"I stay here and get stoned with you, Perry, and your wonderful brother, Shed."

The plaintive lilt of "Macrimmon's Lament" filled the already social back garden of Shed's lodgings in Kilburn. He was a happy man. His brother Peregrine had dropped in unannounced on an impromptu visit, requesting a change of clothing and had brought with him a charming visitor, Pedro, a travelling musician, the most extreme piece of jailbait he had ever set eyes on. And he had an audience as he gave it large on his beloved bagpipes. The day was going well. Feeling quite light-headed after all the skirlin' and birlin' he had been indulging in as he showed off to his guests, Shed sat down.

"Bravo! Bravo!" roared Perry through floods of tears, mightily moved by his brother's fine playing. "Pass that bottle of Cameron Brig Pedro and we'll have another dram for the road. I will not have you disappoint your public on my account."

As it was only a short walk to the venue, they set off at a march with Shed, at full blast on the pipes, leading the way. They entered the bar of The Mean Scotsman to great acclaim, Shed was a regular and well known to the staff and clientele. A stream of off-duty builders thronged round him offering drinks and communicating with him in Gaelic. Shed was in a euphoric state as he laid his pipes on the bar and roared out: "I"ll flash any man in this pub for a fiver!" and raised his kilt. There were no takers, Shed was responding well to a course of Viagra. After murdering his first pint of Guinness he felt refreshed and thought about having another go on the pipes when a pretty girl caught his eye. She looked a bit like Kate Moss. He withdrew from the crowd at the bar and floated over to her table and introduced himself. "Has anyone ever told you that you're a dead ringer for Kate Moss?" he chirruped charmingly.

"I *am* Kate Moss you silly Scotsman! I'll flash you for a fiver!" Shed's bravado had disappeared now that La Moss had called his bluff, and what was more worrying, she was now fiddling with his sporran. He eased his embarrassment by offering to serenade the iconic waif and fled to the bar to retrieve his pipes. He threw them on and launched into a medley of Rob Stewart hits, camping it up outrageously. Backstage in the broom cupboard that passed for a dressing room, Pedro was getting dogs abuse for his disappearance from the other Libertonis.

He waved away their protestations and claimed that he had needed some time alone to get his shit together.

"Anyway I 'ave met zee most splendido musician, can you not 'ear 'im? I 'ave ask 'im to jam, he will open zee set with zee Last Post on zee bagpipes!" Mac Quiz, the manager and a mean Scotsman to boot, asked Pedro if he wanted paying.

"We 'ave not discuss bread, man, 'e eez a superstar."

"I'll have a word", said Mac Quiz, worried that he might have to fork out. "I'll offer him twenty quid."

When he strode into the bar his patriotism was tested. Shed was a blur of tartan and Kate was trying to dance a highland fling on the table. ☻

To be continued...

His Name was Wanker Sam

AND HE WAS LEGEND.

STORY AND ILLUSTRATION BY MARK MANNING

Let me take you down—not to Strawberry Fields, that was in Liverpool.

I lived at the other end of that foetid Northern waterway.

The Leeds and Liverpool canal.

My childhood summers were often spent swimming in its murk skilfully avoiding dead dogs' arses.

Unwanted drowned mongrels, they always floated arse up because of the sack of rocks tied to their collars. Tails still jaunty, poking out of the water like grotesque,slimy reeds, bits of grey, greenish bone showing where the hair and skin had slithered off.

There amongst the rotting fish, rusty bedspring skeletons, stolen bicycles, used johnnys, fag packets, bits of broken polystyrene, sour milk bottles and all kinds of other shit that had been thrown in just to see the splash, I would close my eyes and imagine that I was a pirate swimming in the iridescent, blue seas of the Caribbean.

Then when I bumped into Pongo's dead butt I would quickly realise that I was still in Armley.

The Leeds and Liverpool canal was a magical place for a child.

Despite the filth and frugging hordes of paedophiles paedophiling away all over the fucking place

Paedophiles, man.

There were fucking thousands of them on Armley park.

Whole feral tribes hiding in bushes and lurking beneath railway bridges like demented masturbating trolls, all running around clutching huge sacks full of wine gums, puppies and little kittens.

But of all these wild perverts there was one that stood a whole bell end taller than the rest.

His name was Wanker Sam and he was legend.

"Ouick! Quick!" would go out the cry "Wanker Sam! He's on the park! Under the railway bridge!" The horn was sounded and the hunt would be on.

SAM AND HIS TRIBE HAVE GONE DEEPER INTO THE WOODS

Off we would all race, we barking Sam hunters, up back streets and out across main roads, charging headlong into Armley park and tumbling down the golf course only to discover that once more our cunning and elusive prey had given us the slip.

If we were lucky we might just catch a fleeting glimpse of the fiendish worm-burping Yeti disappearing into the swirling mists that hovered around the banks of the canal.

The usual debris of Sams sordid existence, fag ends and gay wank mags scattered around on the overgrown towpath.

Wanker Sam was a scary yet fascinating figure to the kids of Armley.

A kind of spunkish bogeyman.

Because none of us had actually seen him, but we knew kids who knew kids who had seen him, all kinds of rumours surrounded this strange supernatural masturbator.

His knob was over two foot long, he had pointed teeth and was a cannibal who after bumming kids to death would eat them, use their arse to make his bread et cetera.

Occasionally Sam would be spotted on some obscure stretch of the canal violently strangling his ghastly turkey with one hand while dispensing Embassy regals with his other, trying to lure his prey near enough for him to grab and bugger inside out.

Of course everyone claimed to know of at least one kid who had been caught by Wanker Sam and taken off to his terrible buggery den deep in Bramley forewoods.

Blood curdling tales of anal horror involving eels and baby pit bull terriers circulated around the park about what exactly Sam did to your jacksie if he caught you.

Things are different these days of course, Sam and his tribe have gone deeper into the woods, some people, somewhat optimistically I feel, even believe that Sam's kind are extinct.

Wrong, very wrong.

Not so long ago before anybody really believed that these gruesome mythological creatures existed outside the terrible imagination of Jacob and Wilhelm Grimm, our bumfumbling friends were as free as birds. Free to wander the bushes and canal banks indulging themselves to their hearts content with their sodomistic little hobby.

They would frolic merrily with local kiddies, a joyous song in their arses and not a care in their cocks.

Appropriate job opportunities were myriad.

All kinds of well paid employment to keep themselves and their little friends in wine gums and fags.

Swimming instructor, Boy scout leader, youth worker, ice cream man, Redcoat.

The openings and opportunities where a wanker could indulge his furtiveness seemed endless.

A football coach, a foster parent, why, back in those glorious long gone days you could even bum your own kids and no one said anything.

Ah, to be an arse bandit back in in those wonderful times, what joy it must have been.

To live and be a wanker in an age when old men who took a keen interest in children and their world were considered to be kindly old grandad types with pockets full of Worthingtons and Willesdens cricket almanacs.

What heavenly snake oil delight it must have been to be a Kentucky Fried arsebandit back in those innocent 1970s.

Camping down in the forest singing songs around the roaring fire, bangers sizzling away in the frying pan, up to the nuts in a favourite tenderfoot's bumhole.

But all goods things must come to an end, and sure enough it didn't take long before old Sidney Cooke and his friends at the *News of The World* eventually blew the whole gaffe.

Their symbiotic relationship forged in troughs of equally escalating venality, one for pre-pubescent arse and one for sales figures forced poor Sam underground.

Now everyone knows that all these harmless old grandad, boy scout, childrens home, swimming instructor, church worker types are far more likeley to be keeping jars of industrial strength muscle relaxants in their pockets rather than Worthingtons originals.

Forewarned and forearmed as those altruistic nice people at the *News of the World* would have us believe.

But Sam, he's a cunning beast, it will take more than the kind-hearted concerns of that eminently respectable Sunday newspaper to purge us of the scourge of the perve.

He's still there, old Samuel Intercourse.
A horrible ghost
haunting
the
fizzing
bleeping
undergrowth
deep down in the luminous depths of the cyberforest.
Wanking in his gingerbread house.
Be afraid,
be very afraid,
little children.
Wanker
Sam
has
gone
electric. ☽

THE
PRACTICAL
IDLER

THE PRACTICAL IDLER

Welcome to the Practical Idler, the section of the magazine which invites readers to extend their interest in idling beyond the mental plane and to take it out there on to the physical plane, eventually. This season we offer advice and reflection on growing fruit in the urban garden rather than watching people put decking down on telly, fishing, taking tea, dealing in second hand books and the joys of classic cars. Plus Will Hodgkinson describes the process that led to writing his book *Guitar Man* and Paul Hamilton reflects at fantastic length on the portrayal of kids in the movies.

YOUR GUIDE TO THE EASY LIFE

STATIONERY REVIEW:

FOUNTAIN PENS

Tom Hodgkinson goes with the flow

Sometimes you find yourself doing crazy things. I recently bought a pack of twenty biros in the market, reasoning that this was a great bargain and would mean that we would never again have to hunt for a pen when taking a phone message at home. What a fool I was. In a few days, the biros had virtually all disappeared. After a few weeks, I can occasionally root one from deep inside the drawer, but inevitably when I start to write with it, it simply scratches the paper, and leaves no ink. I shake the darned thing, flick it and wobble it around. Sometimes it writes one and a half words before giving up. Biros also do something awful to your handwriting. They don't go with the flow, they crab your hand and produce an ugly scrawl.

Now, compare this experience with the wonderful fountain pen. Two years ago I bought a very cheap fountain pen which cost about the same price as twenty biros. Somehow fountain pens do not get lost. That's one advantage. There are many others. Firstly, unlike the vulgar biro, fountain pens are a

CHEAP QUILLS: POETRY IN MOTION

pleasure to use. The way the ink flows from the nib encourages the user to produce a more elegant hand. There's no scratchiness; just an elegant transferral of ink to paper.

They look good, too. How much more elegant and stylish to reach for your fountain pen in a meeting than pull a scraggy broken biro from your pocket.

Also, you don't step on them and make a horrible cracking noise. They last for ever; they produce no waste. We should eject all biros from our homes. They are a false economy, a destroyer of beauty and a creator of unrest. But a fountain pen—ah!— truly, a fountain pen is harmony, it permits the free flow of the mind onto paper. It seems that the further back you go technology-wise, the more pleasurable things are. If there is this much joy to be had from transferring from biros to fountain pens, imagine the raptures of delight that will attend taking up the quill! ◉

CHLOE KING

GARDENING:

DITCH THE DECKING

Graham Burnett has better things to do than watch gardening lifestyle shows on telly. Like, nothing.

Lifestyle Gardening? No thanks! Friends and colleagues are often surprised by my attitude towards Reality TV gardening shows—for aren't they are encouraging the cathode-ray addled masses to get outdoors, get their hands dirty and get growing—surely no bad thing? Well, I'm afraid I'm unconvinced. Basically they are just another variation on the endless slew of "makeover" programmes that tell us what to eat, what to wear and how to live. You know the kind of thing—invariably they feature an host of celebrities gurning into the camera whilst they slap down the decking, exotic ornamentals and (ahem) "water features" as a "surprise" for some gormless householder while they'd just popped down the shop for a packet of fags. If these punters couldn't keep their garden in order when it was just a patch of lawn with a rabbit hutch and a kid's tricycle on it, how do they hope to cope once its converted into a high maintenance, Corporate Garden Centre-dependent mini-version of the Hanging Gardens of Babylon?

My vision of the urban garden is a place where we can begin to develop self-reliance, growing useful crops such as fruit, vegetables and herbs by implementing permaculture techniques and methods. The difference between the permaculture garden and its more "conventional" counterpart is basically to do with design—or at least, an approach towards design. Of course,

"design" is very much addressed by the "lifestyle" shows. However this tends to be focused purely in terms of aesthetics and fashion—what colours and shapes go well together this year, where best to place that decking or water feature to impress the neighbours, how to avoid those plants and flowers that are just so passé... It's also an exclusive and top-down approach. We the viewers, as well as their clients in TV land, simply sit back and gawp as open-mouthed passive consumers whilst "The Experts" dazzle us with their skills, knowledge and witty banter.

Permaculture design on the other hand is more about building up a thorough and intimate understanding of both your garden (its aspect, soil type, wind and rainfall patterns, what plants or creatures share it with you, etc) and what you actually want from it. Therefore my first piece of practical advice to any gardener that would

SANDRA HOWGATE

OUR BUSHES AND TREES DRIP WITH GRAPES, CHERRIES, APPLES, LOGANBERRIES, BLACKCURRANTS AND RASPBERRIES

prefer to work with rather than against nature is simply to slow down: "Don't just do something—sit there." Many permaculturists recommend a non-intervening observation period of at least twelve months. In reality this isn't always practical as we usually need (or want!) to obtain some kind of a yield before this, and you might well fancy cultivating at least part of your plot in order to get in a few crops of spuds, onions, carrots, etc. However the "leave it a year" rule is certainly good advice to follow before making any changes that may be difficult to reverse, such as any major landscaping, pond creation, tree and hedge planting or building permanent structures like sheds and greenhouses.

By practising "thoughtful inaction" rather than the frantic activity promoted by the makeover shows you will gain a good solid grounding regarding the relationship between you, your garden, its limitations and its assets. In the long term such

insights will be essential if you are to develop a truly sustainable and integrated landscape that can produce food, medicines, seeds (for propagation or sharing out with others—make your plot a community hub!), craft and building materials, fibres, dyes, and much more.

This certainly isn't to say that productive landscapes should be about visually dull utilitarianism. Form follows function, and all the permaculture gardens I've ever seen are places of great beauty. But this kind of beauty flows from the relationships to be found in natural eco-systems, at once elegant in their simplicity, yet at the same time diverse in their complexity. Furthermore, a well-designed permaculture garden has many other "uses" beyond simply growing stuff—play area (for kids or adults...), spiritual retreat, open-air art gallery, wildlife sanctuary, tree nursery, nattering with the neighbours, yoga and mediation space, bio-diversity storehouse or somewhere to dry your washing.

Above all, the permaculture garden should be somewhere for relaxation and enjoyment, not yet another place to get hung up about whether or not you are "doing it right" or meeting others' expectations. For me, there's nothing like our small urban garden on a summer's afternoon. The bushes and trees are literally dripping with grapes, cherries, apples, loganberries, blackcurrants, strawberries and raspberries, whilst burnet, sorrel, rocket, mints, Welsh and tree onions, chives, lovage, lettuces, day lilies, marigolds, poppies and other edible leaves and flowers fill the salad beds. Buddleia and evening primroses scent the warm air and frogs and newts plop into the pond. Blue tits search the trees for bugs whilst starlings polish off the cherries that are out of human reach. Cuban or dub grooves drift from the open kitchen window and I'm under the shade of the quince tree in a deck chair with a case of fine local beer and a good book—truly the embodiment of "the designer as a recliner", and much better than watching the telly any day... ☻

Graham Burnett runs www.spiralseed.co.uk

THE ANGLER:
SUPER FLY GUY

Kevin Parr on fishing with insects

Sir John Fairclough was a scientist of great note. Instrumental in the development of the early IBM computers, chief scientist to Maggie's mob in the eighties, and a man whose memorial service at St Martin's in the Field was attended by royalty and statesman alike.

He was also a fly-fisherman, though he started late in life and illness overcame him before he had dampened too many flies.

His widow, however, was left with a problem while arranging his estate; how or where to pass on her late husband's fishing gear. It was, after all, barely used, and though its financial value was of no interest to Lady Fairclough, the pleasure it gave her late husband ensured much thought would have to go into its disposal.

She spoke of her dilemma to friends, and asked if they, perhaps, knew of anyone who might be interested in taking the tackle off her hands. They knew just the person, and, overnight, I became a fully equipped, if entirely inexperienced, chalk stream fly fisherman.

I was naturally humbled, though quick to admit to Dr and Mrs Baits that I had never heard of their great friend and my generous benefactor. Nonetheless a door had sprung ajar which I had previously kept firmly shut.

As a coarse fisherman, I have generally regarded fly-fishing as a completely unnecessary and self absorbent pursuit; enjoyed by those people whom in a previous life may have employed me as a chimney-sweep or shit-shoveller.

My prejudice was probably borne during childhood in the trout infested chalk-stream environment of central Hampshire where I grew up. I found it strange, as a boy, why people would make it so hard for themselves in the pursuit of trout, tying flies from feathers to their rods and thrashing the water with them in vain, when a lump of bread caught every fish in the river.

We discovered a by-law as kids which permitted the fishing, for free, from road bridges in Hampshire. In hindsight it was a law blatantly made up by my friend Leigh, but it didn't stop gangs of kids with handlines plundering the Itchen trout stocks. It was such easy pickings that one kid made serious money by selling "local" trout to the teachers at school, and the pinnacle was Leigh's capture of a four and three quarter pound salmon, a fish that required two people to carry it home.

As freezer stocks grew, though, river stocks dwindled, and before long we were catching nothing from the bridges and angling our way back to the ponds.

We had, of course, all but fished the river dry, though the fly-fishermen continued their fruitless art, and, until recently, I

couldn't grasp why.

Now, though, I understand the critical balance of life within a chalk stream. Why for all their stupidity, trout are the only fish capable of populating so many river reaches, and why the care for such environments is so vital to endangered species such as the water vole and white-clawed crayfish.

And, I must admit, I had formed a curiosity for fly-fishing which was just about ready to burst when my unexpected gifts arrived.

With both the desire and equipment, all I needed was a venue.

Kieran rang with impeccable timing. Nell, whose wedding we had attended last October, has a godfather who owns a stretch of the Test. Would I care to join them for a July day?

It was a most stunning body of water. I vaguely knew the area but had no idea that such an expanse of water-meadow and overgrown river-bank existed.

A twenty minute walk took us to the fishing hut where a rather haphazard morning's fishing began. Casting a fly is tough, and with a stiff breeze in my face I tangled my line with almost every cast. Kieran, the only one of us with proper experience, caught a grayling first cast and made the process look easy.

I struggled on, but, after lunch in the hut and a few glasses of Spanish encouragement, set about my task with renewed hope.

Wading upstream I rose a fish but spooked at least a dozen. I had two boxes of flies and steadily worked through them all but with no fish rising they were wary and unimpressed by my efforts. At the upstream point of an island I found a fish in slack water. My third cast brought a take, but I pricked the fish and it surged out of site.

Despite the loss, I was encouraged by the brief contact and a little further upstream found another fish and carefully waded into position below it.

After perhaps my twentieth cast, rain began to fall. We had endured showers all day but this was set in.

AFTER A FEW GLASSES OF SPANISH ENCOURAGEMENT, I SET ABOUT MY TASK WITH RENEWED HOPE

I got wet. I fished on, and after at least a hundred casts at the same trout the line lay as perfectly across the surface as if I had placed it by hand.

This time he was mine.

I have caught some big fish in my life and lost even bigger ones but never have I played a fish so carefully as this trout that I knew was not even a pound in weight.

And it is many years since a capture has meant so much to me as that fish—my first fly-caught trout.

I ran down the bank to show the others my prize. Running, partly due to my excitement, but also because this fish was going back alive, it was too important to die, and, in all honesty, wouldn't have fed a cat.

It was a day of firsts, and a day for openmindedness, and as we sat by the pub fire an hour later I held a glass to my fish, and to John Fairclough, a generous man I shall never meet. 🐟

ANTHONY HAYTHORNTHWAITE

TEA TIME:

THAT FIRST SIP

Chris Yates recalls the bike crash which led to his first ever experience of tea

The first sup of tea I remember is not associated with anything pleasurable, in fact, such were the circumstances, it's a wonder how I came to be so firmly attached to a teapot.

I was about eight or nine and I was riding home on my bicycle after walking all the way to the bike shop where it had just been repaired. It had a new front brake, but in his former life the bicycle repair man must have been a child murderer because, as I was whizzing down the last hill before home, the nut securing the brake mechanism to the forks came off. The calliper jumped forward, jamming the wheel, somersaulting the bike, flying me through the air for quite a long way before I came down face first on the road. A car screeched to a halt behind me; I heard someone running towards me from the house on my left. A woman spoke to me, helped me to my feet and led me, bleeding and dizzy, into her kitchen while the car driver ran off to fetch my mum.

As I was being daubed with cotton wool soaked in Dettol, I remember the woman saying how a nice cup of tea "with extra sugar" would do me "the power of good". By the time my mum arrived I was sitting, bandaged and sore, but holding a mug and sipping my sweet, curious tasting medicine. It was so sweet it was sickly, yet there was also something about it that made me feel whole again and I knew I might have to try another cup when I got home.

Within a year I'd become a regular tea drinker, though, fairly soon, I'd discovered that it tasted much better unsweetened. My parents used to buy their tea in bulk direct from the importer—John

Dron—and the standard (loose leaf) Ceylon made a very fine brew. It was so good, in fact, that I was sometimes disappointed by some of the tea I was offered elsewhere. When you're young, senses are so much sharper and more sensitive than in later world-worn years, so that if someone pours you a cup of stewed tongue-rasping metallic Typhoo, you feel perfectly within your rights to call the police and have the place closed down.

I once lost a good friend because of a poor cup of tea. Jeffery used to go to my school, but then moved on to another "better" school and I was only able to see him when I was invited over to his house for tea. Tea, however, was not readily available as Jeff and his pals never drank it, preferring orange juice, and his mother never thought to offer me a cup. Then a day came, after we'd been playing for hours in the woods behind his house, when all I wanted in the world was tea, and I asked Jeff to get his mum to make me a pot.

She seemed a bit peeved as she came into the living room

CLARE HATCHER

OUT NOW

THE NEXT IN OUR CRAP SERIES:

the Idler book of

CRAP HOLIDAYS

Edited by Dan Kieran

WARNING
ADULT CONTENT

50 TALES OF HELL ON EARTH

BRINGING TOGETHER 50 CRINGE-MAKING TALES OF
WHAT HAPPENS WHEN THE DREAM HOLIDAY TURNS INTO
A NIGHTMARE.

STARRING: FAMILY DYSFUNCTION AND FALL OUT,
HURRICANE-BATTERED CRUISES AND BLISTERING
SUNBURN, INAPPROPRIATE HOLIDAY AFFAIRS AND
EMBARRASSING STDS

later, where cakes and sandwiches were already laid on a table, carrying a tray with a metal teapot and the usual extras. She clumped it down on my place mat, I thanked her and she left us to it. I poured myself a cup, and after pausing to savour the moment, took a sip.

"Urgh!" I said. "This tastes like dog pee!"

At that same moment, Jeff's mother came suddenly back into the room and I went suddenly red faced and silent. It was obviously the perfect excuse never to invite me back.

But even my mum's tea, when it had been swilling in a Thermos flask all day and we were sitting on a beach eating tomato sandwiches, could sometimes taste like dog's pee - though usually, if I was out in the open air and offered a cup of tea, any blend of tea, it would taste divine.

The best cup of tea I can remember from childhood was made from an unknown leaf brewed in a catering-sized teapot at a stall by a bus stop on the outskirts of Walton-on-the-Hill. With two mates, I'd been on an epic bike ride in the rain across Headly Heath and as we rolled into Walton we caught the scent of toasted buns and spotted a plume of steam rising from the front of a wooden stall. The words "Tea and Cakes", in big white letters never looked so seductive. We didn't have quite enough pennies for three cups, but as it was the end of the day, the tea lady took pity on us. She also had a half finished packet of chocolate digestives which she gave us for nothing more than the promise to come back another day.

Though it was the last pot of the day, the tea was fresh and delicious and we sat on a bench in the mild spring rain and realised you didn't have to die to go to heaven. ◉

THE TEA WAS FRESH AND DELICIOUS AND WE REALISED THAT YOU DIDN'T HAVE TO DIE TO GO TO HEAVEN

PASSENGER:

DRIVE ME CRAZY

Fanny Johnstone celebrates getting hitched by hiring an Austin Healy

Like most girls I always wanted to get married before I had actually found a man worth marrying in the first place. I suppose I should be very embarrassed about this as it's a bit like saying I want to be famous without actually having anything to be famous for. And. Oh. Oh dear. Excuse me while I stuff that copy of *How To Be Brilliant* underneath my mattress and turn off the karaoke machine. But hang on a minute: are girls alone in growing up and wanting to share their lives with someone? No. Most of us grow up wondering whether we might fall in love with someone who feels the same way about us. And in our deepest darkest moments of self doubt the notion that we might holds us tight and drives us forwards.

Anyway, God knows I've had enough proposals and put enough poor men through the ringer before finally getting around to actually doing it. Happily, and finally, it was to the right man. He might not think so, but two months after the wedding do I really care?

But wait! I showed I cared on our wedding weekend by doing all the things that I thought a bride-to-be or a new missus should. These included looking as gorgeous as I possibly could, telling him how much I love him and getting him an 1965 Austin Healey 3000 Mark III for him to run around the country lanes in.

I'd like to say that it was my Katherine-Ross-Does-Woodstock style, and the delectable ratio of my bosoms, waist and hips that had him weeping with love on our wedding day but I think it might have had more to do with the car. By then he was so in love with its ice blue and white curves and its

damn husky engine that I barely got a look in. Tuh. Just as well I didn't get him the scarlet E-type•.

I had a choice you see. Oh yes. Which just goes to show that beggars can be choosers, depending of course on what scale of begging we're talking about. But if, like me, you're the sort of unfamous (not even infamous) beggar that can't afford the £20,000 to buy the car in the first place then the answer (whispered tones) is to hire it. And as we were getting married on the Lizard Peninsular in Cornwall I hired the car from a very nice and funny man called Rob Constant.

Rob owns Cornwall Classic Car Hire and he has a mouth-watering fleet of cars which you can hire by the day or over a weekend. The idea is that you jaunt around Cornwall in one, perhaps referring to his beautifully written information pack to help you find the best Cornish beauty spots (mine's above my left tit, boom boom), and possibly helping yourself to the delicious hamper stuffed full of organic Cornish goodies on the back seat.

This might sound a bit like an

AH... THE CAREFREE DAYS OF SUMMER

advertisement for Cornwall Classic Car Hire but actually what I am trying to tell you is that driving a classic car for a weekend was just one of the most magical things in the world we ever did and here's why.

When we picked the car up on the Thursday morning before our wedding we couldn't believe how the world seem to transform. I know this sounds like pre-wedding loved-up waffle but this is what happened. We got in the car and, just like entering into a beautiful room, felt ourselves framed by quality and character. The car had an interior that immediately transported us back to the sixties. As we purred along (and boy did we purr) time seemed to slow down. Everyone else rushed past at the usual 21st century rate but even though we were comfortably doing 70 mph with the hood down nothing seemed urgent or stressful, not even lack of cake or the occasional traffic jam.

Was this because people waved at us and smiled instead of flipping the bird as usual? Or because we had dressed for the part and so felt the part· Colin in a beautifully tailored sixties suit and me in a spanking yellow retro sou'wester and high-heel sixties boots? Was it because, as we drove along, we sung our hearts out to tracks like the Kinks' "You Really Got Me Going" and "For Your Love" by the Yardbirds? Or was it because knowing that our wedding weekend was about to start was the happiest and most exciting moment of our lives? Of all the things we wished for as kids, this dream was coming true and there we were, driving towards it in the Healey together, the notion holding us tight, the sun dappling through the trees, the horizon bright and clear. ◉

Cornwall Classic Car Hire:
www.cornwallclassiccarhire.co.uk
0845 458 1108
National Car Hire Guild:
www.hchg.co.uk http://www.hchg.co.uk

BOOKS:

TRIALS OF A BOOK-HUNTER

Kirk Lake deals to support his habit

"I s there anything that you're looking for in particular?"

It's a familiar question. The real response is that I am looking for something that has been underpriced, that I can buy very cheaply and sell on quickly for a healthy profit. But what I'll actually say is "No, I'm just looking".

If somebody asks me what I do I can't bring myself to say bookdealer. I just dislike the word dealer with its connotations of drugs or, worse still, antiques. And bookseller is just as bad; somehow quaint and safe, reminding me of tweed and small market towns where too many people are wearing Wellington boots. So now I am going to try the title book hunter. Like hunting and gathering; man versus book. The laconic browser. Lee Marvin in spectacles.

It wasn't always like this. Once upon a time I was your everyday bookshop browser, aimlessly searching for something new and unusual. Not really a collector, more an accumulator.

Then I saw a 1955 paperback of *The Ginger Man* which was marked up at £2. I quite liked the novel. But I didn't need it. I'd already read it.

I bought it anyway. I knew this was the first edition and it was worth, at the time, over £200. The Olympia Press paperback of *The Ginger Man* became the first of many thousands of books I have bought with no intention of reading.

Book hunting for profit is getting increasingly difficult as more and more local bookshops either close or move all of their stock online.

There's nothing more disheartening than seeing a neat little pencil code next to the price on a book. This is the mark of the internet and it fills the book hunter with dread. Wherever the codes appear you can be sure there will be few bargains to be found. Each book will have been checked against the vast dealer database/marketplace at www.abebooks.com. The knock on effect of this is that bookshop stock across the country will be priced, more or less, the same.

Whereas once the onus was on the owner to maintain a knowledge of his stock and develop areas of expertise leading to specialized shops and niche markets today there's no need to pass on any books at all.

TWO JAYS IS ONE OF THE FEW REMAINING BOOKSHOPS IN LONDON WHERE EVERYTHING ISN'T ON THE INTERNET

Horse breeding or player pianos, military history or needlepoint embroidery—the Internet is the great leveller. Everybody can find a price for every book.

A customer from my old shop was bemoaning this very point. A retiring CID officer who bought books by Nietzsche and Baudelaire and anything we could find about LSD. He professed a love for Krautrock and Fairport Convention. We called him "Hip Cop". He was a prime time television detective series in waiting. I'm sure James Nesbit was already on standby.

Hip Cop told me about Two Jays Bookshop in Edgware. One of the few remaining shops in London where everything isn't on the Internet. An old-fashioned shop where the stock is priced relative to what it was bought in for.

Though I'm shooting myself in the foot here, I recommend Two Jays to every aspiring book

hunter or even to that dwindling breed who buy books to actually read rather than as a tradable commodity.

The shop is well stocked, the prices are fair and there are no pencil codes to put you off.

Edgware is near to Elstree. Maybe this is why Two Jays has a good selection of film and theatre books.

But then, like the false theory that a charity shop in a rich area has classier items, a bookshop's proximity to affluence doesn't necessarily translate into quality inventory.

Another shop with the benefit of uncoded stock is the bookshop in Flask Walk, Hampstead. Now this should be brimming with book gold. Only a hundred yards from Peter Cook's old house, right in the heart of the country's literary premier league. But inside it's chaos. There can be good books here but you certainly have to hunt them down. It's claustrophobic and confusing. Towers of books closing in like a lost library level of Doom.

In the past few months I've bagged this book bounty from these two shops alone: A 1935 book on ice hockey; an Arne Jacobsen catalogue with a postcard from Arne inside; an early 1970s promotional leaflet for the Whitefriars glass factory; Walker Evans, *The Americans*, first edition from 1938 with no dustwrapper; signed books by George Best, Steve Hislop, David Hockney and Margaret Thatcher; two hardcover copies of Nick Rhodes' photography book *Interference*, terrible photos but tremendously popular in Japan and the USA.

I paid a total of £65 for these books. Want to know how much they might be worth? Try abe. Want to buy one? I'm open to offers. ◉

Two Jays Bookshop 119 High Street, Edgware, HA8 7DB (020 8952 1349)
Keith Fawkes Bookshop 1-3 Flask Walk, Hampstead NW3 1HJ (020 7435 0614)

BOOKS:

ESSAYS IN IDLENESS

Mark White sits back with a Japanese classic of lazy literature

You can't trip over a tabloid these days without reading about schoolkids torturing each other while filming the action on their mobiles, indulging in after-school orgies, popping pills like so many psychedelic smarties or vying for the most nonsensical ASBO. The modern-day school system is clearly failing its charges, and could well do with taking a leaf from the *Tsurezuregusa*, one of Japan's set school texts, written in the 14th century by Zen Buddhist monk Yoshida Kenko. The book's title is usually rendered as *Essays in Idleness*, though a closer translation is "Leisure Hour Notes"—an intoxicating source for philosophy, with much relevance to contemporary life, and a whole lot better than the current set texts of dog-eared copies of *Heat* and autobiographies from former *Big Brother* contestants.

Kenko's *Essays* is a collection of 243 different meditations of varying lengths, from etiquette through drunkeness to passionate love and the fleeting nature of life, whilst always finding room for the right approach to existence—doing as little as possible. "I wonder what feelings inspire a man to complain of 'having nothing to do'," he wrote. "I am happiest when I have nothing to distract me and I am completely alone." He goes on to warn of the dangers of conforming to society's mores: your mind can be corrupted, you have to watch what you say, you're always looking for an edge. "Intoxication is added to delusion," he wrote, foreseeing a million Saturday nights, "and in a state of inebriation the man dreams. People are all alike: they spend their days running about frantically, oblivious to their insanity."

Kenko's solution to the insanity of modern life—and remember this was written more than 650 years before the Blackberry, Crazy Frog ringtone and 24-hour news channels—is to cut out as much of the frantic stuff as possible. In words familiar to the idle, he noted: "Leaving something incomplete makes it interesting, and gives one the feeling that there is room for growth." The Imperial palaces of the day always had a room left unfinished, after all, and Buddhist and Confucian philosophy texts were only complete when they missed out chapters.

"The pleasantest of all diversions is to sit alone under the lamp," he wrote, beautifully, "a book spread out before you, and to make friends with people of a distant past you have never known." It also starts to explain his motives: Kenko's lazy

> "THE MAN WHO FAILS TO KEEP IN MIND THE PRECIOUSNESS OF TIME IS NO DIFFERENT TO A CORPSE"

because he's thought about it, not because he's foolish and short of options. "To engage in useless activities, to talk about useless things, and to think about useless things during the brief moments of free time left us is not only to waste this time," he wrote, "but to blot out days that extend into months and eventually into a whole lifetime. This is most foolish of all... a man who fails even for a short time to keep in mind the preciousness of time is no different from a corpse. If you wish to know why each instant must be guarded so jealously, it is so that a man inwardly will have no confusing thoughts and outwardly no concern with worldly matters; that if he wishes to rest at that point, he may rest, but if he wishes to follow the Way, he may follow it."

The mention of the Way is more than a nod to Taoism, the philosophy that says humans should move effortlessly through

life, never exerting themselves more than a flowing stream that hugs the ground as it passes. As the *Tao Te Ching* explains: "Do that which consists in taking no action, and order will prevail." Kenko argued that simplicity and humility, the ways of the sage, are the surest routes to happiness. By really wanting something to happen, you will naturally be disappointed when for whatever stroke of bad luck your plans go wrong. Far better to flow through life unencumbered by possessions, both mental and physical. "Some things are probably indispensable to daily life," wrote Kenko, "but as for the rest, it is probably best not to own anything at all."

Kenko was born Urabe Kaneyoshi, the son of an administration official. After an early career as a court official he became a monk aged 41 following the death of the emperor Go-Uda in 1324, changing his name to Yoshida Kenko. Authorities differ on whether he retired from public life, as his essays often comment on the loss of beauty from the world so are still part of it—Japan in the 14th century was a turbulent place, with the collapse of the Kamakura Bakufu, the attempted restoration of the Emperor Go-Daigo and the confusion of the Northern and Southern courts. It does seem, though, that any interest in the outside world was from the perspective of the hermit. The *Tsurezuregusa* began its slow ascent to its status as a Japanese classic in the 17th century, when the first detailed commentary on it was published and the work adopted as a basic element in teaching the young an honourable way of living. It's been unchallenged in that position since. More than 100 editions with commentaries were published in the two decades following 1945, for example, and Takashi Saito's *Essays in Idleness for Everyday Life*, updating Kenko's thoughts for the present, was in Japan's Top Ten best-selling books in early summer 2005.

Kenko teaches us to live each second fully and to appreciate that each moment makes our short lives worth living. How much more important an

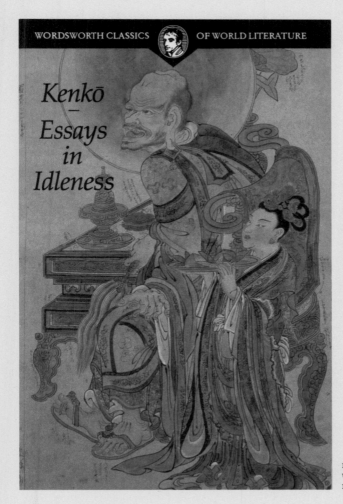

WORDSWORTH CLASSICS OF WORLD LITERATURE

Kenkō — Essays in Idleness

KENKO TEACHES
US TO LIVE EVERY
MOMENT TO THE FULL

approach, then, than to run around in the cacophony and noise that passes for most of mass culture of whatever age. "In all things," he wrote, "it is the beginnings and the ends that are interesting. Does the love between men and women refer only to the moments when they are in each other's arms? The man who grieves over a love affair broken off before it was fulfilled, who bewails empty vows, who spends long autumn nights alone, who lets his thoughts wander to distant skies, who yearns for the past in a delapidated house—such a man truly knows what love means." And also how an idle nature can bring anyone through the rockiest of bad times. Now all we need is to get Jamie Oliver interested, the book in every classroom, and the school system will fall like a ripe plum into our outstretched hands. 🍃

EASY SOUNDS:

GUITAR MAN

Will Hodgkinson wields his axe

A few years ago I did an interview with Graham Coxon, then on the verge of leaving his old band Blur and starting out as a solo artist. Being a guitarist had treated Coxon well: he lived in a large Victorian house on one of Camden's prettier squares and wasn't doing much beyond looking after his young daughter and re-cataloguing his CD collection. I arrived to find him enthusing about J Mascis, the former guitarist of the American post-punk band Dinosaur Jr and almost always described as one of the most indolent men that has ever lived.

How could this be true? Playing guitar had always looked like work to me—all those evenings spent practising chords and scales with so much effort for so little return—and it was hard to understand how the leader of a hard-touring cult rock band could be described as lazy, particularly when he was so admired for his guitar style.

"But it is a lazy thing to do, isn't it?" countered Coxon. "You sit on the sofa for an afternoon and strum a guitar and you slowly get better without actually doing much. It's not like going out and working for a living. You put the kettle on, smoke a cigarette, strum a guitar as a vague idea of a song forms in your head..."

It was only then that it dawned on me. The guitar is the sword of the workshy. It has rescued generations from decades of toil, the only caveat being a lifetime of financial insecurity and painful fingertips. The rot usually sets in during adolescence, when learning the solo to Sweet Child O' Mine becomes more important than homework, family mealtimes and life itself. Then it spreads into young adulthood, by which time most guitarists have joined bands in which their creativity can be let loose. If public success

follows it's usually down to the ambition and hard work of the lead singer, allowing the guitarist the space to bask in the glory of being petulant, misunderstood and true to their art. Then, if you're lucky, you can announce yourself to the world as a guitarist until it's time to die.

A year ago I picked up the guitar at the embarrassingly late age of thirty four. Although I've left it a little too late to use the instrument to get out of working, it has still changed my life—for the better. It is the most accessible instrument in the world. Anyone can do (something) on the guitar in a matter of days; it doesn't take long to learn two chords and get a rhythm going between them, or to master the chord of E and be able to play most of The Ramones' back catalogue by moving the E-shape up and down the neck. The £100 I spent for a cheap Chinese production line model proved adequate for my novice needs; for a beginner, there is little point in spending more. In order to force myself to practise I set a goal: to perform a gig in front of a paying audience after six months. It seemed like a good idea at the time; after all, the 60s band The

WILL EVEN
FOUND SOME
SHOES THAT
MATCHED HIS
GUITAR

JOHNNY MARR TOLD ME THAT ALL YOU NEED TO PLAY GUITAR IS LOGIC AND EXCITEMENT

Small Faces had their first hit six months after Steve Marriot started playing.

The six-month mission involved getting lessons and advice from guitarists I admired. The message that rang out across the disparate voices of my tutors was this: enjoy it. While some of those I spoke to were rock stars that had found fame and fortune through their dedication to the guitar, nobody thought of it as anything like work; nobody even seemed that interested in the career aspects of being a musician. Roger McGuinn, whose jingle-jangle 12-string guitar on The Byrds' hits like *Eight Miles High* and *Mr Tambourine* helped soundtrack the 60s, admitted that he had never bothered to learn to read music, or ever studied his craft with any real diligence; he had simply learned to play guitar because he loved old-fashioned folk music, and he had stuck with his jingle-jangle sound for the last 40-odd years because that's what he enjoyed playing and "people seemed to like it".

Johnny Marr, who revolutionised guitar styles in the 80s with The Smiths, told me that all you need to play guitar is a combination of logic and excitement, before spending the next hour presenting to me his mastery of the lead riff to *Gimme Danger* by The Stooges that he had learned when he was 15. The former Stooge that had come up with that riff, James Williamson, had long given up degenerate rock'n'roll for a career in computers; his son described the guitars that still lined the Williamson family's living room in Silicon Valley, California as "the coffins in the corner". After badgering Williamson constantly for an interview and finally getting one, it was nice to hear that he picked up a guitar for the first time in a decade after our various conversations, and found his way around his killer riffs once more.

The Idler's own blues guitar god John Moore explained that his entire adult life and devotion to the guitar had been shaped by two things: having a cool uncle with a collection of rare blues albums, and meeting Bo Diddley at the age of 16. I tried to interview Les Paul, the man that invented the solid-body electric guitar and was still playing midnight sessions in a New York jazz club every Monday at the age of 89. However many questions I asked him, though, his entire philosophy of the guitar boiled down to one word: "practise".

My guitar odyssey led me to some of the most exciting and unusual people I have ever met. In the poor, dull, crack-ravaged town of Greenville in Mississippi I met an eighty-six year-old blues guitarist called T-Model Ford who only picked up the guitar at the age of fifty when his fifth wife left him. He had been on a chain gang for murder, and in State penitentiaries more times than he could remember (when I asked him how many times he had been to Parchman Farm he replied: "I don't know. How many?") He had spent most of his life working as a logger in the Mississippi woods and as a petrol station attendant in Greenville. His wife gave him a guitar and amplifier to fill the space that her leaving him would create, and as he sat at home and worked out how the thing worked the night she walked out, two women visited his house. Impressed that he had a guitar and amplifier, both slept with him. The following day he chucked in his jobs and has never looked back. Since then T-Model Ford has released records, travelled the world and contracted gonorrhoea, although his knowledge of geography has not improved much since he left Mississippi for the first time for his first concert outside of the State. Two years ago he announced himself to the crowd of his concert in Canada with the words, "Hello, Germany!"

Then there was Teddy Paige, a former session musician for the fabled Memphis recording studio Sun where Elvis Presley, Johnny Cash and Jerry Lee Lewis were first unleashed onto the world, who had jacked in his life as a top blues guitarist to become a medieval troubadour in Europe. He dressed up as a jester and survived by playing his guitar and lute from country to country. It had all been going well until 2000 when Teddy ended up in a council flat in Hastings and took exception to his neighbour playing techno. Teddy expressed his anger in a rather authentically medieval way: he hacked at his neighbour's arm with a sword. When I last saw Teddy, it was within the sterile lime green walls of a maximum-security psychiatric institution in Sussex. But he still had a guitar with him, and it was getting him through what must otherwise have been a pretty horrible time.

The most inspiring guitarists that I met were Bert Jansch and Davey Graham, the key figures of Britain's 60s folk boom and both extremely singular men who used the guitar as a passport to an exciting and itinerant, albeit financially Spartan, life. In 1960, when he was 19, Davey Graham had written a beautiful instrumental for his then-girlfriend called Anji that became the rite-of-passage tune for every budding acoustic guitarist to master, and Bert Jansch had adapted and developed Anji for his own. My goal was to play a version of Anji at the gig, and Bert Jansch was the first of the two I tracked down. A shy man who was more articulate through the guitar than he was through words, Jansch was generous in taking time to show me the building blocks of Anji, and he revealed himself as someone that had used the guitar to do exactly what he wanted to do.

Jansch loved folk music but had no interest in the change-resistant traditions of the folk scene; his heroes were Davey Graham, who ignored any notions of purity in music, and Jimi Hendrix; anathema to the average folkie. Jansch was the most practical of my mentors, teaching me to do acoustic techniques like alternating bass lines and claw-hammer, but through example he showed me how being a professional guitarist could involve staying in bed until midday, spending afternoons with a cup of tea and a guitar, and going out to play in front of an audience—it didn't matter to him if he was playing in front of 10 people in a pub or before a sold-out audience of London's Royal Festival Hall—in the evenings before getting back home by two or three for a good nine hours of sleep.

Davey Graham was harder to find and proved to be, when I finally tracked him down, a much wilder character than Jansch. The son of a Guyanan mother and a Scottish father, Graham had grown up in 50s London and first picked up the guitar in his teens, quickly becoming obsessed with it. Interested in the connections that existed, in Davey's mind at least, between traditional English music, Indian classical and North African Berber music, he travelled through the South Of France, Morocco and India in 1959 and 1960, using his good looks and his guitar as his ticket. Liz Taylor

ROBERT JOHNSON · ROGER McGUINN

GUITAR MAN

A SIX-STRING ODYSSEY · OR YOU LOVE THAT GUITAR MORE THAN YOU LOVE ME

THIS MACHINE KILLS MY FINGERS

JOHNNY MARR · BERT JANSCH

WILL HODGKINSON

going to the pub. He would come back, turn the record over, and go to the pub again. Then he would return and ask for £10.

Nobody seemed to know where Davey was, least of all Bert Jansch, with whom he had a love-hate relationship that had recently erred towards the latter emotion. Finally I managed to find him: he was living in a barren flat in Camden. A rusting iron camp bed, a wheelchair stolen from his last visit to hospital, a nylon guitar and a mandolin were all that filled the space between the dirty yellow walls of his bedroom. Trying to get him to show me how to play Anji was hopeless. He opted instead to demand to be taken to the pub where he expounded on a complex theory about how Greensleeves was the focal point for western music. The monologue was cut short when the sound of *Roll With It* by Oasis blasting out of the pub stereo induced a dramatic panic attack and he marched outside. We went back to the flat, where he rolled one joint after another before standing in the middle of the room with a beatific grin on his face, strumming his mandolin as he stared at the bare light bulb hanging from the ceiling. Here was the greatest living British guitarist, strung-out, signing on, and transported to another dimension. Davey's world still seemed infinitely more attractive than, say, his millionaire one-time disciple Eric Clapton's Armani suit-clad one.

A year on from picking up the guitar, I find myself playing my acoustic most evenings when the kids have gone to bed. It's a more inspiring way to relax and clear one's mind than watching television, and it amazes me that I could spend the rest of my life with these six strings and never exhaust their possibilities. And the guitarists that excite me are the ones that have found freedom through the instrument, whether that is in Bert Jansch's quiet way or Davey Graham's wild adventures. I would recommend the guitar to everyone. As long as you don't think of playing it as work, you will be hooked for life. ◓

Guitar Man by Will Hodgkinson is published by Bloomsbury

spotted him busking in Paris and brought him to the Riviera to play at her parties for a summer season. By the time he returned to England in 1961 he was a legend, as worshipped for his inventive playing as he was for his glamorous persona and the fact that he only rarely turned up to his own gigs.

Davey's untameable character gave his expression free reign, but it caused problems. He was hooked on heroin by his early 20s and has suffered drug addictions and mental health problems ever since. In the 80s he was reduced to living on proceeds from guitar lessons, his unreliability meaning that people stopped paying him for concerts he didn't show up to or albums he didn't make. These lessons were said to consist of playing his students one side of an album by Ravi Shankar and

EASY SOUNDS:

SOUNDS OF THE SUBURBS

Jean Emmanuel Dubois **meets** *La Caution*

Don't believe the hype! A vision of suburbia from its residents, Radio HDR (for Hauts de Rouen, or Hills of Rouen) is the symbol that something positive can come from the French suburbs despite what some "generous souls" may say. Founded by Moïse Gomis, Radio HDR was created after the riots that took place in the Rouen suburbs in the late 90s. Rouen is a typical French provincial town with its sleepy bourgeoisie on its right bank, named the historical centre, and the rest, the left bank and its suburbs, being the working class "enfant terrible". Well, with 50%

VOICE OF THE YOUTH

unemployment rate it's not a surprise that Rouen's suburbs are filled with frustration. So it was a big deal when a *Time* Magazine journalist noticed the radio station's existence. It was like a seal of approval that was a long time coming from the local French press. The British press was quite amazed by the concept of associative radios as this kind of thing didn't exist in the UK. The main goal of a radio station like HDR is to give back to people the possibility to express themselves. With its no-ghetto, free access politics HDR aims to teach the suburban population how to use the media tools that they are deprived of most of the time. People are brainswashed with French mainstream media like TF1 with their FOX News-like sensationalist aesthetic, a station that was keen on feeding the "sentiment d'insécurité" (feeling of insecurity) of your average Jean (Joe). Therefore helping both Jean-Marie Le Pen to be on the rise and Nicolas Sarkozy, recently with the French riots, to use the same

LA CAUTION ENJOY A NICE CUP OF TEA AND A SIT-DOWN

language. So radio stations like HDR are a breath of fresh air, a proof there's still media by the people for the people.

Nikkfurie & Hi-Tekk are two brothers living in Noisy le Sec (93) a Parisian suburb. With their unique kind of rap under electro influences, their flow and their references (RUN DMC, Public Enemy, the Wu Tang Clan and the writer Philip K Dick) the duo is easily standing above the rest of the French rap world without the stupid macho pose or low brow lyrical content sometimes associated with that certain kind of rap. One of their tracks, "Thé à la menthe" was chosen by Steven Sodenberg himself for *Ocean's 12*. They are also currently working with the underground film maker collective of Kourtrajmé hosted by director Kim Shapiron with all the support of French & international film star Vincent Cassel. So even if

you do not understand a word of French or if rap is not your thing you should give La Caution a try. The two brothers don't choose easy shortcomings and are people who read and think a lot. As they are living in the middle of what was called "the french riots" by Fox News & co it was a chance to have a point of view without clichés or easy sensationalist effects. Let Nikkfurie talk:

"*Peines de Maures,* the title of our album, is far from being innocent. The general protest we are seeing is the result of social frustrations we are trying to describe. It set fire to the suburbs and to the "difficult" areas, most of the time with the district 93 as a starting point, our suburb, where 18 storey buildings are plenty. After the death of the two young people electrocuted and the tear gas hand grenade in the Mosque, Sarkozy wanted to "ban" these "punks", by sending CRS cars, CRS teams being very well known for their tenderness. The result was easy to tell. The hatred toward the police is not dating back from yesterday, it is the result of the disturbing similarities, especially ethnic ones - that exist between the kids from the suburbs and all the poor ones killed by police bullets.

So, the media hold guilty all these Frenchmen with North African and Black African origins. The politicians exult because at elections "the arab, the black" is a recipe that gives votes! And it has been that way for a long time. Televisions & newspapers have vomited in arrogant and subliminal ways, for more than 50 years, and are the referees in the race for power in the country of human rights! We have been, one after another insulted as being "natives, clandestines, hooligans, punks, terrorists" and so on.

So, loads of youngsters do not believe anymore in any social system, the French one just needs them for want of something better, they have no link anymore with the country they came from. Integration will

THIS COUNTRY IS ALMOST OURS — ONLY ALMOST

not be the dish of the day as long as prejudice toward Arabs and blacks feeds guzzed ballot boxes, in favour of the Sarkozy, Chirac, Le Pen & other De Villiers. Otherwise, what was the point of integrating such an openly islamophobic man as Claude Imbert in the "Haut conseil à l'intégration" (sic) ? How can such an islamophobe think of integrating muslims?

This country is almost ours, only almost. But that's not enough to get a large part of the suburban youth losing their faith. Suburban people who are studying and working two times harder than their fellow "white" countrymen, but are drawing a particularly strong self sacrifice from their social situation. It is the same in the artistic or sports worlds where strong will, experience, and personality are literally "doping" the talent to turn it into genius. As a matter of fact don't we say: Zidane "the child of the Castellane suburb?" As if to underline that the place he came from helped to forge one of the best soccer players of all time.

As some of these young people are dropping out of society, others don't give up and are getting diplomas. These latter people are a light of hope in these areas, in the way that they will be tomorrow's bosses and that the logic of job discrimination will only be a bad memory! We, La Caution, think that the best answer to that underlying racism, is to get out of this social morass (that the elite don't want us to leave, not for the world) that leads to social protest, and to take profit from these difficulties and turn it into motivation and go foward." 🔊

Nikkfurie (La Caution) La Caution: Peine de Maures/ Arc en ciel pour daltoniens (Kerozen music/Wagram) www.la-caution.net

TRAVEL:

ISLANDS

Matthew De Abaitua goes it alone

To The Edge Of The World. The vision of an island, coming out of the fog as you approach it by boat, or surveyed from a beach on the mainland, is alluring. What is the promise of an island? Isolation? Certainly contemporary fears stoke in all our hearts a secret desire to hide away, with a good few miles of water between us and them. An island promises untapped resources. Fantasy Island. Treasure Island. Stand on the cliff and look out at the promise of an island, and you understand some of the urges that drove the ancient peoples to make perilous sea journeys to them.

The myth of a Great Flood appears in many cultures, not just in the story of Noah in the Old Testament. The Aborigines of central Australia say that in the Great Flood, man retreated to the mountain tops. Hawaiian legend tells of a time when the sea entirely overcame the land, aside from one peak on Maunakea, where two people were spared. In the Great Flood, mountain tops become islands. The peak of Ararat where the Ark tottered is the Ur-island, the point from which Man started all over again.

As soon as you land on one island, you are hunting on the horizon for another. There is always another island. This is an ancient rule. When hopping between the islands of the Western Isles and Outer Hebrides, I read of an axe-head discovered in the moorland of Lewis, dating from somewhere between 3500 and 3000BC, the late Neolithic Age. The material it was made of— porcellanite—is found in Northern Ireland, suggesting that there was trade between the Lewis and Ireland. Trade across two hundred miles of Atlantic Ocean, with no map, no lighthouse, no lifejackets! Was the prospect of a barter solely what drove the ancient peoples to make such a trip, or was it the irresistible prospect of landing on another isle.

Admittedly in 3000BC, the climate of the Western Isles was warmer and drier than it is today. This was before the climate change of 1500BC, when higher rainfall waterlogged the soil, turning it into recalcitrant peat. The islands were more bucolic, these treacherous prehistoric journeys from isle to isle make more sense if you reckon in a more hospitable climate, a more fertile soil. Isn't that a prospect? A fecund virgin isle (for some reason, islands stoke my libido—we'll consider that question in more depth later, unless you prefer to draw a discrete veil over it now). Once the Western Isles became clad with peat, it was harder for the crofters to scratch a living. As Dr Samuel Johnson remarked in his *A Journey To The Western Islands Of Scotland*, the islands of the Hebrides have little to recommend them unless one is a "mere lover of naked nature".

CLOCKWISE FROM TOP: 1. LOOKING FROM FROM IONA TO MULL. 2. THE MANDALA GARDEN ON THE BUDDHIST HOLY ISLAND 3. HOLY ISLAND FROM ARRAN. 4. ROCK PAINTING ON HOLY ISLAND

THISTLES IN THE GARDEN OF THE ABBEY AT IONA; FARMHOUSE ON THE ISLE OF SKYE

(There—you see—his sexual turn of phrase shows that even Dr Johnson felt the stirrings of isle lust somewhere below his enormous gut.)

The endpoint of Dr Johnson's journey was the spiritual island of Iona. Boswell, his traveling companion, was very keen to visit the isle, supposed burial place of the Kings Of Scotland and the point from which St Columba spread Christianity to the wild highlanders. Iona is a mere kerb of land off the coast of Mull, reached today by a small ferry from Fionnphort. It is an island just beyond an island, a hop and a skip from the mainland. This makes traveling to Iona feel even more like an adventure.

When I visited, on September 11th 2001, the beach at Fionnphort was riddled with jellyfish, a dozen flesh Frisbees.

Down in the narrow sound, fishing boats meditated at anchor. The silence was prehistoric. The ferry to Iona is full of Catholic pilgrims to the sacred isle. It pulls up by a line of whitewashed cottages and the island's fine hotel The Argyll. The stone of Iona is rich in iron, and at sundown the Argyll looks like it is constructed out of chunks of steak, with the mortar resembling the marbling of fat. Take the rainslick Street Of The Dead through a ruined nunnery and you come to the grounds of the Abbey. Sitting out as the last of the light lurks above the distant hills of Mull, one feels negligible. A bystander in the eternal war between the sea, the sky and the rock, that red rock, stained with the blood of Oran, a pictish convert buried alive in the foundations of the Abbey by his friend St Columba. When the burial was done, Columba decided he wanted to see the face of his friend one last time. Heaving the earth aside, he found Oran still alive and uttering such blasphemous descriptions of heaven and hell that he was briskly buried once again. There is a lot of flesh in the rock. The Kings of Ireland, Scotland and Norway were buried here. The island is a grave, opening into the great void of the Atlantic.

There is always another island, another stepping

stone. At Iona, just as I was smugly downing malts in the bar of Argyll, enjoying that edge-of-the-world frisson, I learnt of the remotest inhabited island in the British Isles; the isle of Foula, separated from the Shetland Isles by fourteen miles of ocean. A place so remote that its people still observe the Julian Calendar, celebrating Old Yule on January 6th with the New Year not beginning until January 13, and so storm-tossed that the ferry has to be winched out of the water in case it is dashed against the harbour. One of its sea cliffs rises to over 1200 feet, topped by a rock platform that hangs over the abyss, a natural diving board. It is this cliff that features at the opening of Michael Powell's film *The Edge Of The World* about the evacuation of St Kilda (Powell wanted to film on St Kilda but it proved impossible so Foula stood in for it). Two young virile men race to the top of the peak to decide whether they will abandon the island or not. But one of them, taking a short cut, doesn't make it and falls to his death.

The loss of a young man is catastrophic to the community, unleashing the forces that will lead them to abandon the isle. At its peak, St Kilda supported two hundred people. By the time of its evacuation on 29 August 1930, the population was down to thirty (after an outbreak of smallpox in 1720, Foula's population was down to three). In Powell's film, the modern world in the form of trawlers provide too much of a lure to the young people. Also, they lack the medical resources to care for a young baby. In Powell's fiction, the islanders leave the place "were life as our fathers knew it is no longer possible".

S t Kilda had been inhabited for 4000 years. Go and find a map. Look how far out it is! One hundred and twelve miles west of the mainland, forty one miles west of the Outer Hebrides. Sea storms would isolate it for nine months of the year. How far out could you go there? Mentally, that is. And socially. Is that the libidinous appeal of the island? Being cut off from normal propriety? Perhaps an adolescent viewing of *The Wicker Man*, set on the fictional

DOWN IN THE NARROW SOUND, FISHING BOATS MEDITATED AT ANCHOR

Summerisle, where every young lad was obliged to lose their virginity to Britt Ekland, is the crucial influence here. Yet, with their low populations, on these islands you were obliged to breed. Urgently breed. And young men are wanted, needed, for survival. Teenagers are useless in cities but on islands, they are the ones who can climb down the steep cliffs to fetch the puffin's eggs for breakfast (at least that was the case up to the 1930s).

In my imagination, Foula is a terrifying place, a mist-shrouded rock with Atlantic winds speeding you over its sheer cliffs. As Samuel Johnson noted, the monks had a habit of building their retreats in the most beautiful of spots, and they never really bothered Foula. That there is one further island than Foula, the abandoned St Kilda, the two bound together by Michael Powell's film, makes me shiver.

The rule that there is always another island first struck me on the isle of Arran, which is further south than the Western Isles, directly west from Glasgow in Argyll. While staying in the southernmost pincer of Lamlash

HOLY ISLAND FROM ARRAN

Bay on Arran, I looked out at the enormous hump of Holy Island, (not to be confused with the more famous Holy Island of Lindisfarne) and plotted a trip there. It was a few days before the boat resumed its run to the island. In Lamlash's Co-Op, the alpaca wool of my hat attracted the interest of a Buddhist monk. He too was keen to get back to Holy Island. His partner had recently died. Together they were responsible for striking rock paintings that dot the path around the island. He pointed to my hat and asked me if I had been to Tibet. I hadn't.

"Tibet is not an island," I replied.

He looked confused.

"I only go to islands," I explained.

In order to become a Buddhist monk, one must undertake the long retreat of three years and three months. Certainly this man, I think his name was Christopher, had the spacey air of a man who spent a lot of time on a remote island. Watching him navigate a supermarket, I coined the simile of "looking as pained as a Buddhist in the Co-op, trying to chose between Flora and I Can't Believe It's Not Butter." The aisles enforced bathos on this head-in-the-clouds islander. He was sullied with earthly concerns, with brands and images. Yet he needed it. He needed it for his toast.

For three days, Holy Island remained coy under a habit of cloud. I sat on the beach, angry with lust for it. At moon rise, its silhouette was that of narrow waist and voluptuous hips. The wing beats of gulls ricocheted across the bay and at dusk, the seals lolled in the shallows, turned their tails up and watched me sulk. The world turned within me, moved onto the next tooth of the cog. Finally, the skirt of cloud was hitched up, inviting us in, and we were able to take the boat across the bay.

The Holy Island project began in 1992 when the island was purchased by the Rokpa Trust. The peace centre on the North of the island is open to people of all faiths, so long as you adhere to the five golden rules; while on the island, you are requested not to kill anything, not to steal, not to lie, to refrain from booze and fags and, finally, hold off having a shag until you are back on Arran. The peace centre is on the retreat circuit. I overheard two walkers discussing the inevitable politics of communes as they had arisen in the various retreats they had embarked upon. Nothing I heard made me change my opinion that all communes are doomed to acrimony over lentil allocation. Just to walk around the island was retreat enough for me. A path takes you from North to South, where there is an International Women's Buddhist retreat, then turns over the low hump of the peak and back down the other side. Along the walk, there is a mandala garden, a grove of young trees planted for the lost children of Dunblane, a hermit's cave, and a few striking, colourful rock paintings of Buddhist icons.

Retreat is a possibility modern man worries about on a daily basis, the way you tongue a cavity and consider the dentist. No one wants to be suburban. You want to live extremes. Either be the junction box through which all the currents of the metropolis flow, or live in a fucking cave on an island a few miles out from another island. The condition of contemporary life—its incessant chatter, its deprived public space—turns our faces once again out to sea, in search of peace.

Against such romantic idealizations, there are the realities of island life. As Samuel Johnson wrote of Talisker on the isle of Skye: "Talisker is the place beyond all that I have seen, from which the gay and the jovial seem utterly excluded; and where the hermit might expect to grow old in meditation, without possibility of disturbance or interruption."

In *For The Islands I Sing*, a fragmentary autobiography by the Orkney writer George Mackay Brown, he considers the sea valley of Rackwick on the isle of Hoy—"a green bowl gently tilted between the hills and the ocean". "We must always be on our guard not to romanticise: life in a place like Rackwick must always have been stark and dangerous and uncomfortable."

Islands have been used as prisons. Consider Alcatraz or its forebear, the prison isle of Chateau D'If off the coast of Marseilles. It was on the Chateau D'If that Dumas imprisoned The Count Of Monte Cristo (even in Dumas' lifetime, sightseers journeyed to the isle to see the cell in which the Count was held, and so one was constructed, along with a hole from which the character supposedly escaped). It is a forbidding construction. The boat drops you at the base of a rock staircase zig-zagging up the side of the stark fortress. The sun hammers away at the anvil of your skull. You get off the boat and immediately want to get back on again.

Still, we are people of extremes. Could we not cope with the privations of island life, especially as we would now have a few tricks of modern technology up our sleeve? Let Mackay Brown spell out our case for becoming an islander:

"Yet I believe that their closeness to the elements, their pursuit of whale and herring and their anxious tending of the corn all summer, the winter flame on the hearth that their own hands had dug from the moor, while—if the harvest of sea and land had yielded an adequate bounty—the cupboard was well stocked till spring; that kind of life is more meaningful by far than the lives of people who set out each morning for an office by train with *The Times* to read; a holiday in Spain with wine and sun the only oasis in their desert." ◓

FILM:

THE CRAPPIEST DAYS OF YOUR LIFE

Paul Hamilton on kids in the movies

The deplorable exploitation of children in sweatshops and Rio Tinto Zinc mines has been rightly exposed for the degraded and vile business it so obviously is. Disgusting too is the psychological damage wrought on child stars. The likes of Judy Garland, Mickey Rooney, Drew Barrymore and Elizabeth Taylor are testaments to decadent upbringing by both film studios and collusive parents, intent on wringing the last dime out of their babies before their balls drop or sprout wizard beards. Certainly, the adult Rooney is funny in It's *A Mad, Mad, Mad, Mad World* and *Pulp* but his apoplectic, shrieking, babbling, psychotic, hyperventilating turns are surely a pointer to the neurotic paranoiac that Hollywood made of him. He and Taylor's gruesome catalogue of marriages betray either an insatiable addiction to wedding cake or, more likely, a belief that people are puppets, toys to amuse them and are summarily broken and discarded when they've grown bored.

The root cause of this, perhaps, is that adults do not understand children. How a child can bear to watch a video of the same film over and over again is a flummoxer for the parent. Yet they too were once children. What happened to cause this break in understanding? The sixteen-year-old boy looks at his box of soldiers and monsters and he can't get back to the mindstate he had some eighteen months before when he could spend hours playing at war or blowing up the universe. Something decisive and awful happens with puberty or maybe the first pint of lager: You are indulging in a grown-up's pastime and with that first lager-tainted piss, you piss away the mysterious magic of the childhood imagination. Thereafter, you no longer have your own worlds in your mind. Instead, you become reliant on the manufactured dreams of others, becoming obsessed by pop groups, film stars and poets. Where once you were actively running your own race, you have become a participant. One way to test the post-piss change is by watching again a film you loved when you were ten or so. Re-viewing it, you will undoubtedly be pondering,'What was so magical about this rubbish? I used to roll around in front of the telly crying with laughter at this! It's just mindless crap.' But it's not mindless crap, really: You are. As adults we lose the capability of pouring ourselves totally into a film. Now we have to know beforehand what the critics and our friends think of it. We check the DVD box for the running time and give the plot blurb a scan to see if it is our 'kind' of film. In short, we clip our wings. Rather than throw ourselves into the strange new worlds of pictures and song and bend our heads accordingly to accommodate them, the adults demand that the mountain come to them. Crabby blinkerism: So often we hear the moan of 'Why should I go to that art exhibition/gig/screening? What's it got to say about my life?'

Film directors, almost without exception, are balefully ignorant of the child's nature. Invariably, they are depicted as adults-in-waiting. The disgusting Disney films are populated with passive, redundant-except-as-plot-devices kids (Mowgli in *The Jungle Book*, those prim dullards of *Mary Poppins*) whose sole purpose is to gawp at funny or frightening big 'uns. Disney calamitously reduced *Alice In Wonderland* in the same facile manner, Alice's character rendered thinner than a card. It took Jonathan Miller with his 1966 version to restore the essential childlike essence of Alice. In Miller's revolutionary back-to-the-roots telling, Alice is sarcastic, wrong-footed, bored, prone to introspection (lost in her thoughts whilst lost in Lewis Carroll's thoughts). Miller captures a child's reaction to the March Hare's Tea Party by resisting the temptation to play it for laughs. As the novelty of the occasion wears off, the action and dialogue slow to a crawl and a chronic, inescapable, empty English Sunday afternoon turns eternal.

The empty Sunday afternoons of my adolescence were filled amiably with the immortal shambolic caricatures of humanity in the various shapes of Irene Handl, Miles Malleson, Ian Carmichael, Sidney James, Michael Ripper, Margaret Rutherford and Uncle Alistair Sim.

Rutherford and Sim co-starred in the 1950 hit *The Happiest Days Of Your Life*, playing the respective head beaks of opposing single sex schools forced to share the same buildings and playing fields. Produced and directed by Frank Launder and Sidney Gilliatt with the economies of the post-war austerity—cardboard sets and stolid, basic camerawork—the mystery is simply whose happiest days is the title referring to exactly? The

FILM DIRECTORS, ALMOST WITHOUT EXCEPTION, ARE BALEFULLY IGNORANT OF THE CHILD'S NATURE

pupils of Nutbourne College For Boys and St. Swithin's Girls' School are, but for an enthusiastic pillow fight in the dormitory, well-behaved and anonymous. The action centres solely on the frictions between the male teachers (including Guy Middleton as caddish Lothario and sports master 'Whizzo' Hyde-Brown) and their female adversaries (with quarter-to-three feet Joyce Grenfell as Whizzo's opposite number). The enjoyment in *Happiest Days...* for ten-year-old me was there in recognising adult archetypes I saw my own school teachers— the ancient somnolent French master, the vague, bookworming Science master, and, especially, the bone-domed owlish Richard Wattis as the cynical wag ('I love monotony') of a gambling-obsessed Maths teacher. Cruel fun—and children's humour is unapologetically sadistic—is extracted from the long-suffering school caretaker, the geriatric Rainbow, being worked to death—hauling hundreds of heavy trunks, continually erecting and then removing

CLOCKWISE FROM THE TOP:
TIN DRUM, *Les Quatre Cents Coups*, THE HAPPIEST DAYS OF YOUR LIFE, KES

rugby posts according to the whims of Sim and Rutherford.

In 1954 Launder and Gilliatt returned to school for the first in their increasingly dire *St Trinians* series, based on cartoonist Ronald Searle's justly celebrated cartoons of wicked, unruly schoolgirls, a battalion of sawn-off horrors armed to the teeth-braces with catapults, hockey sticks, stink bombs and knuckle dusters. With the scratch of a nib Searle allows you into the cunning mind of these devious damsels, on the look-out for dangerous fun and hang the consequences (and the school cat, too). Launder and Gilliatt lack Searle's inventive genius—like most adults, they have little understanding of how children are, their impulses, their reactions, their tastes—and so the pre-teen St Trinians girls are flatly rendered; a straight copy of Searle's school uniform and outsize tricorn hat, invariably with the pupils also sporting black-as-your-hat mad caveman wigs. Launder and Gilliatt have no interest in children and so Searle's original stars are relegated to the status of extras. They have a deeper fascination for the teenage girls at the school. Bottle-blond bouffanted, gravity-defying breasts jutting like a dead heat in a zeppelin race, languorously pulling on ciggies or putting on lipstick, the St Trinians gaol baiters are scheming and avaricious; Flash Harry (George Cole), the spiv who lurks in the school grounds, operates a dating agency for them, marrying them off to oil sheiks and sugar daddies. He is their pimp, in fact. Oddly, although L & G strike the expected moral tone elsewhere— horse thieves and train robbers always finish up wearing the steel bracelets—the pimping of underage girls goes unpunished. L & G are more concerned with contriving as many opportunities as possible to have their harem of fishnet-stockinged, micro-skirted lovelies go up and down ladders. Fifty years on and little has changed. The films of Larry Clark (*Kids*, *Bully* etc) share L & G's salivating voyeurism, and there's something deeply contentious in a middle-aged film director ordering his child actors to perform violent or sexual acts on each other for the benefit of his all-seeing camera. The glossy, vile manipulation of children is not solely a male preserve: *Thirteen*, a look at the fascistic pressure on American schoolgirls to conform to a narrow delinquent mindset of slutmeat for classmate acceptance, is directed by Catherine Hardwicke with brio and verve, until the scene where the wannabe-hipster Evan Rachel Wood is given a French-kissing lesson by her mentor-in-cool Nikki Reed. Then, the hand-held cameras swoop and zoom in on the snoggers like a Ben Dover masturb-piece. (Hardwicke is seen on the DVD of *Thirteen* being interviewed, her middle-aged face framed by exceeding silly braids. Why do Americans in particular fear age? Why do they cling so ridiculously and pathetically to some twisted ideal of youth and beauty? So pervasive is the poison of vanity and the cancer of Cool, it's even claimed Bob Dylan as a victim of self-delusionism. On his late 2005 British tour he was barely a silhouette of a shadow, so dim were the stage lights, and, perusing the concert programme, there were plenty of large clear close-up photos of a 24-year-old Dylan but only a couple of recently captured blurred monochrome distant shots. Like Ma in his "Maggie's Farm" song, it's 2005 but he thinks it's '64.)

More disturbing than the calculated-to-shock teen piffle of Larry Clark or the taste-lapses of *Thirteen* is the sexualisation of pre-teen pupils in the Jack Black vehicle *School Of Rock*. The story is hoary; it's the old bilge of how, against all odds, a loser can confound his so-called betters and win. In this instance, Jack Black—he of the Mexican-waving eyebrows—is a heavy metal guitar-playing anorak and obnoxious retard who, kicked out of his band and needing big money to pay big rent, finagles a job as a teacher to a class of bright but deeply staid, middle-class, conservative ten-year-olds. Plotting revenge on his treacherous ex-band, Black transforms these bright but dull showers into a rock band in his own image, and enters them into a Battle Of The Bands contest with the dual intention of instant fame and instant riches (his eyes are on the prize money).

The ironical joke of *School Of Rock* is that it takes a egomaniacal, paranoiac, middle-aged man to instill into sedentary, studious, *Village Of The Damned*-living-dead ten-year-old children the essence of wild abandon and—Black's mantra—'sticking it to The Man'. The deeper irony, of course, is being a headbangin' rock'n'roll motherfucka from hell is a completely acceptable rite of passage into American adulthood. It's their equivalent of national service: See how the attitudes of the band's parents change from disapproval and disgust to pride and joy when they see their spawn rocking out at the Battle Of The Bands show.

Where *School Of Rock* becomes dangerous is in its depiction of Black's class being sexually aware. One boy in the class elects to be the costume designer, creating an array of androgynous clothing for the group. He states a preference for show tunes and Liza Minnelli—the joke being he is an archetypal camp couturier. This sexualisation of pre-pubescents is alarming, redolent of paedophiles' claims that their victims are compliant. Is it a submerged compulsion to taint beauty, to corrupt innocence, to shoot out the light? Is this the core reason for the child abuser's obsession, to take a pure and defenceless child

and then inflict lasting mental and physical hurt?

When Ken Russell's film of The Who's rock opera *Tommy* was released in 1975 it was castigated by rock critics as a betrayal of the spiritual purity and idealism of the original record, and by film scribes as being typical Russell—i.e. overblown, glitzy, episodic, decadently banal. Thirty years on, pop music is aural wallpaper, lifestyle commodity rubbish, mindless and meaningless, and film is CGI weariness, blockbuster boredom. Like Nero and Caligula, we have grown jaded by the ever-eclipsing spectacle. Now it is possible to see *Tommy* as it really is, possibly the last great British musical (go on, try and name a better one: *The Wall*? *Absolute Beginners*? Yah-ha-ha-ha!), certainly one of the most imaginatively dressed and designed films. Beneath the welter of surreal imagery—the air raid scene with scantily-clad dancing girls running for cover, their faces decorated by gas-masks, a baked beans-and-chocolate-sauce-smothered Ann-Margret riding a giant sausage, the syringes, snakes and poppies of the Acid Queen sequence—is one of the most tender and sympathetic portraits of childhood aloneness, confusion and inarticulate despair. Six year old Tommy is

TOP LEFT: THE DICTIONARY OF NATIONAL CELEBRITY
BOTTOM LEFT: ST TRINIANS
RIGHT: JACK BLACK IN SCHOOL OF ROCK

rendered deaf, dumb and blind from the shock of witnessing the killing of his father by his mother's lover. (A similar childhood trauma beset Alfred Hitchcock's *Marnie*. Killing a sailor with a fire poker during a confused scuffle between him and her prostitute mother, Marnie grows to be a psychologically damaged kleptomaniac and sexually frigid. Caring husband Sean Connery decides that what she needs is a good old seeing-to rather than a course of head-shrinking, and duly rapes some sense into her.) A series of tableaux detail the inability, frustration, resentment and anger of Tommy's mum and step-dad in their dealing with Tommy's total withdrawal. At a Christmas party, grown-ups and mites revel and cavort in their cracker headgear and plastic copper's helmets, but Tommy, impassive, sits in a toy car in the middle of the living room. The merrymakers attention drifts to the crippled boy but, unlike Tiny Tim in *A Christmas Carol*, Tiny Tom elicits no sympathy, no tears for his plight, only rage that his presence is spoiling the party. The children mock Tommy by marching around him banging drums and then blasting toy trumpets at him, whilst the

TOP: KEITH MOON
BOTTOM: SCENE FROM TOMMY

pissed and glowering father figure, Frank (Oliver Reed, that juiciest of hams, nimbly traversing the tightrope separating self-parody and self-revelation), hides his impotent anger and hatred behind a jolly Santa Claus mask—an ingenious comment on party politics. In the midst of this cacophony comes a break in the clouds and we hear Tommy's interior voice, plaintively asking them to 'See me, feel me, touch me, heal me'. Tommy's unheard appeals are perverted with the emergence of Cousin Kevin—who, under the pretence of babysitter, subjects the boy to a vile litany of sadistic tortures—and the scum-oozing kiddie-fiddler Uncle Ernie. Ken Russell avoids and defuses the true horror by exchanging the child Tommy for the adult model and turning the rape scene for sick laughs. Keith Moon is at his outrageous best as Ernie, limbering up for X-rated exertions with a couple of flamboyant tugs on the chest-expanders attached to his semen-stiff trews. Should there ever be an award for Most Hilarious Paedophile, Moon would definitely qualify in a dead heat with Peter Graves' Airplane pilot. Uncle Ernie is a pantomime pervert due to Moon's childlike exuberance and penchant for clowning, but this is no bad thing. Many of Ronald Searle's most devious St Trinians torture sketches were directly lifted from drawings he made as a captive in a Japanese prisoner-of-war camp.

Since Launder & Gilliatt made such a thorough bollocks-up of Searle's meditations on schoolgirls perhaps it's a relief nobody attempted to film his male rival and successor to St Trinians, Nigel Molesworth, the self-styled Curse of St Custards. Who, though, could have played the philosopher king Molesworth? Had there been a time machine, Graham Moffat—the insouciant, roly-poly, cocky, grudgeful teenager sidekick to Will Hay in half a dozen Thirties comedies—would have been perfect, but by the 1950s Moffat had forsaken the ignominious world of acting and struck out to seek fame and fortune flying model aircraft and running the Swan Inn at Braybrook, near Market Harborough.

Will Hay had toured the music halls with his pince-nez and mortar board idiot schoolmaster act for over a decade before transferring it (extremely successfully) to film. A solo star comedian, he is however best remembered as the inept ringleader of the trio comprising himself, Moffat and wizened, solo-gnashered, glassbacked Moore Marriott, a British Marx Brothers. Hay would try to get his slacker subalterns to pull their socks up and pull their fingers out but the whip he cracked was made of dust.

A typical Hay school farce, *Good Morning, Boys* (1937), serves as a splendid surrogate-Molesworth-could-have-been. Unlike the *St Trinians...* fiascos, the pupils are well to the fore of the action, and it is pleasing to note the great art of miscasting is well-represented, with half of the schoolboys sporting impressive baldspots—a fine tradition that extended until the Sixties, where Cliff Richard's eponymous chums in *The Young Ones* are all knocking the 30-year mark. Moffat's an impressive slackadaisical, cunning bully, he and his gang of delinquent rowdies smoking, boozing, gambling and roughhousing. Their school has been entered in a competition, the first prize being an all-expenses-paid trip to Paris. Upon discovering that Will Hay's job rests upon the competition results, Moffat wrests power from the master, telling Hay to steal the exam paper and do all the swotting-up himself. For their part, Moffat and his pals will turn up at the examination hall and copy down all his work (scribbled away on the inside of eye-patches and alongside shirt-sleeves) and defeat the boffins of competing schools by filling their ink-wells with disappearing ink and other wizard wheezes. Jubilant in Paris, the boys go on the rampage in the bars and nightclubs, nonchalantly catapulting missiles at the cabaret's acrobatic acts when not slouching over their high-voltage drinks and omnipresent, everburning coffin

nails. For all their refreshing obnoxiousness in the face of adult authority, the boys suddenly, and disappointingly, turn law-abiding and patriotic when a criminal parent has 'alf-inched the Mona Lisa. Sure, there was the reward fee for the painting's recovery to consider, and Moffat's mob are a devious and graspy-handed crew, but more than that, there is a definite line drawn in the boys' moral code.

Of course, the 1930s schoolboys anarchy-up-to-a-pointishness is anachronistic to today's Uzi-wielding, ASBO-branded nipper because then Britain ruled the waves, whereas now we waive the rules. 'We're not savages,' claims desert-island-stranded head chorister Jack Merrydew to his fellow public school mites in Peter Brook's 1964 film of William Golding's *Lord Of The Flies*: 'We're English! And English are best at everything. So let's have lots of rules!'

Lord Of The Flies, for anyone who didn't have to suffer this insufferably wrong-headed tome in Eng. Lit., is the (probably incredibly deep and metaphorical) yarn of how civilized children will transform into grunting, bloodthirsty savages if they are transplanted from their comfy cucumber sarnies and croquet surroundings to the jungle. When the boys are first washed ashore from their crashed plane—these chinless wonders being the privileged evacuees from a European nuclear war—they try to maintain the sense of order, balance and fair play instilled and caned into them by their masters. Meetings are called 'assemblies' and a piece of beach debris, a conch, takes on the significance of Parliament's woolsack, for whoever holds the conch is permitted a right to speak. ('Conch' is Golding's extremely clever metaphor for 'conscience'.) Merrydew and his little choir form themselves into a hunting party, dressing themselves in grass skirts and warpaint, and have a fine old time killing pigs. This is their toy soldier games come to life, but it's crucially their means of survival. To appease the nightmare-suffering infants who fear a monster that shares the island with them, Jack mounts a pig's head on a stick as an offering to the beast. This leads to ructions with the 'sensible' boys who view this as worship of false idols and rule by fear. The token working-class kid, an overweight, bespectacled boy lovingly nicknamed 'Piggy', is the pragmatist and realist ('I don't believe in no ghosts ever'), is vocal in condemning Jack's going native and abandoning the rules he initially insisted on. 'BOLLOCKS TO THE RULES!' retorts Jack triumphantly and takes off, his jolly band of butchers skipping behind him.

Golding is a sanctimonious, sentimental, liberal bore in painting Jack Merrydew as the villain of the piece. It's clear that Merrydew is the saviour with his adapt-or-die perspicacity. Jack is an outright bully but what is wrong with that? Bullying is an essential and welcome part of childhood. So many entertainers owe their success to the selflessly enthusiastic bully. A chat show is incomplete without some comedian reflecting that they had to be funny at school lest they incur the wrath of the bully. How many comedians say, 'I got where I am today by bullying the lower years with my witticisms and bon mots?' Lindsay Anderson's *If...* includes a splendid moment of oik-baiting. In the dinner hall, a bully passes along the question 'Biles, why are you such a freak?' down the line to the unfortunate, pale-faced, greasy-locked junior Biles. The boy who finally delivers this honest query to Biles is fit to burst with laughter as he utters it to to the sour-faced shagspot.

Lord Of The Flies ends with the boys being rescued, the upright white socks of the naval officer contrasting with the woad-patterned sprogs. Seeing how far they've deviated from English notions of normality causes them to break down in shame and guilt. What a dismal cop-out! Jack should have speared this authoritarian fart in the heart and had him slowly roasting on a spit. The actual conclusion is inevitable because of film-makers' obsession with children seeking father figures. The notable deviations from this norm are *My Life As A Dog*, where our little hero is disturbed by lack of parental stability (his sole parent is a manic-depressive mother, prone to screaming fits and stay-in-bed withdrawals: This elicits no sympathy from her son since all children are solipsistic and naturally averse to anyone to steals the limelight from them), and *The Tin Drum*, where three-year-old Oskar (supernaturally brought to life by David Bennent) decides his parents, uncles, aunties and indeed all grown-ups are liars, cheats, cowards, bad hats and rotten apples, and so contrives to throw himself down a flight of stairs in an attempt to resist adulthood and maturity. He survives the fall but never ages another day beyond his third birthday, parading through the years bashing seven bells out of his ever-present toy drum and performing his party trick of glass-shattering squealing. (Oskar is a Teutonic tot version of Jack Black in *School Of Rock*.) It's pleasing to see the pastimes of German children. Whereas pre-TV British children would wile away the days tripping up the muffin man or a game of knock-down-ginger, their Prussian counterparts boiled pots of urine soup for the weaker street urchins to taste.

Billy, the boy hero of Ken Loach's 1969 landmark *Kes*, has no father and, like Oskar, views grown-ups as a baleful, uninspiring bunch (his mum is a selfish sluttish sot, his older brother—whom Billy has to share a single bed with—is a pit-worker dullard) and seeks emotional release and temporary escape from surrounding mundanity and drudgeful no-future in flying his pet kestrel. His school is a haven for institutionalized sadism with its cane-happy headmaster and its mini-Mussolini games teacher inflicting cold showers. There is the subtle difference in the bullying procedure in this working-class Comprehensive school and its public school counterparts. The schools of *If...* and the Will Hay films offer thrashings as an incentive for boys to toughen themselves up as future commissars of Big Business and upholding the British Empire. The school in Kes utilise beatings to keep children firmly in their place, to knock the stuffing of dreams out of them. The dorms of *If...* are decorated by the boys with news clippings, pin-ups and postcards, indicating their awareness that there is a real, other world beyond the school

MANY ENTERTAINERS OWE THEIR SUCCESS TO THE SELFLESSLY ENTHUSIASTIC BULLY

gates. In *Kes*, Billy's house is sparsely furnished and nothing adorns the classroom walls, reflecting ubiquitous creative poverty and barren career prospects. It is only when Billy—beautifully played by David Bradley—wanders the woods, whipping the plants with a stick, that the weight of oppression flies from his shoulders like his beloved bird. The deeply powerful Albion-pastoral score by John Cameron soars in these scenes, like the wounded romanticism of Robert Kirby's orchestrations for Nick Drake.

Les Quatre Cents Coups (The 400 Blows), Francois Truffaut's 1959 rumination on the unhappiest days of his life, shares the delinquent aloneness that permeates *Kes*. Twelve-year-old Jean-Pierre Leaud plays Antoine, the only child and silent witness of a claustrophobic, unhappy marriage. He listens helplessly to his parents' nocturnal bickering and is confused, disgusted and betrayed by his mother's sexual infidelities. No tin drum to

paradiddle away his despondency, no kestrel to release his woe, Antoine resorts to skiving off school, losing himself at the afternoon flicks, in the bar football game in a cafe, on the fun fair rides. Rather than fake a parent's sick note, Antoine returns to school with a King Hell excuse for his absence: He tells his tutor that his mother has died. The repercussions are catastrophic. His parents arrive at the school, livid at their son's deception, and Antoine is shamed before his classmates when his father slaps his face. In a cinema-verite sequence an audience of five-year-olds are secretly filmed by Truffaut, captivated, enthralled, spellbound and entranced by a Little Red Riding Hood puppet show. The toddlers are mesmerised, utterly gripped, by the fairy tale, but for Antoine the age of innocence is already over. A career in larceny and deceit is cut short with his detention in a juvenile delinquency centre in the country. Antoine makes an escape bid and runs, runs, runs for all he is worth. But what is he worth? He reaches a beach and only stops running when the sea laps his feet. There is nowhere left to go. The final shot has Antoine turn and face us and all we can do is look back at him.

If boys are merely the predestined mini-moulds of future captains of industry or cannon fodder, girls are simply mothers-in-waiting. Jenny Agutter, in both her most famous films, the extraordinary *Walkabout* and the enchanted *Railway Children*, is the elder sister who has to take charge, assume the responsibilities of a mum. *The Optimists*, a criminally unknown film made on location in the dingy Nine Elms area of London casts red-tressed Donna Mullane in the Jenny Agutter role of big sis Liz, looking after little brother Mark (six-year-old John Chaffey) whilst their parents toil their lives away. Listless with nothing to do and nowhere to go (Liz is first seen drawing a train in the condensation on the kitchen window—an unconscious image of escape), they watch a ukelele-strumming busker going through his ancient patter and sentimental songs in the high street, aided by his begging dog. Gradually they form a friendship with the busker (Peter Sellers) but, this being 1973 Britain and not mawkish Hollywood, it is a spiky relationship. It transpires that this dittyfying derelict is Sam Hall, once a huge music hall star, but now, just like the music halls, obsolete and abandoned. Hall talks in riddles, non-sequiturs, punchlines to forgotten jokes. He mocks Liz's premature seriousness and encourages Mark's fantasising and curiosity. Sellers' Hall is a hall of mirrors, however; each quip is a warping of a hidden regret, echoes of distant losses (his fame, his fortune, his family). He resists the role of father figure—Liz and Mark's dad works double-shifts at Battersea Power Station; his rare appearances at home are bad-tempered, authoritarian (he's simply too tired to show his kids any love)—although they embrace him as such. He is wayward, unpredictable and petulant Like Alfredo the old projectionist in *Cinema Paradiso* who knows he must reject his adoring protege Toto, Sam Hall shuns the children. They must come out of his shadow before they become tainted by his private darkness. Matters come to a head when Liz and Mark take Sam's dead dog into the dead of night to bury her in the pets' graveyard in Hyde Park. Their father, in searching for his children, finds a drunk and distraught Hall who, in a moment of clarity, drops the doublespeak and tells him straight: 'People like you bring kids into the world—you don't know what they're all about. All you can say is "No, no, no you can't , no, don't do that, don't do that, you can't. YOU CAN! That's what it's all about—you can! It's not about filling their bellies up with bread and butter. What about a bit of bread and butter up here? That's where they need it, you know. A bit of the old glass ball! A bit of magic, a bit of dreamboats going on in here...'

Anthony Simmons, the writer and director of *The Optimists*, allows us a rare peek into the psyche of the child. He didn't resort to clever-clever Spielbergy shortcut tricks like keeping the camera three feet off the ground to attain that crucial child's eye view. Rather, his achievement was in the realisation that children are sponges, soaking up the world around them, and then interpreting it all in their own unique, original way. If the son truly is the father of the man, what a stroke of genius it was to cast Peter Sellers, that most childlike of adults (the recent, brilliant Geoffrey Rush biopic of *The Life And Death Of Peter Sellers* is a testament to his poor, demented parenting). At present, *The Optimists* is unavailable on DVD and somehow that is very apt. The secret world of children remains so to the uncomprehending adult. ◉

THIRTEEN YEARS, 36 BACK ISSUES

1: August '93
SOLD OUT
Dr Johnson
Terence McKenna

2: Nov~Dec '93
SOLD OUT
Homer Simpson
Will Self

3: Jan~Feb '94
£8.00
Bertrand Russell
Charles Handy

4: April~May '94
SOLD OUT
Kurt Cobain
Matt Black

5: July~Aug '94
SOLD OUT
Douglas Coupland
Jerome K Jerome

6: Sept~Oct '94
SOLD OUT
Easy Listening
Richard Linklater

7: Dec~Jan '95
SOLD OUT
Sleep
Gilbert Shelton

8: Feb~Mar '95
SOLD OUT
Jeffrey Bernard
Robert Newman

9: May~June '95
SOLD OUT
Suzanne Moore
Positive Drinking

10: July~Aug '95
SOLD OUT
Damien Hirst
Will Self

11: Sept~Oct '95
£4.00
Keith Allen
Dole Life

12: Nov~Dec '95
£4.00
Bruce Robinson
All Night Garages

13: Jan~Feb '96
SOLD OUT
Stan Lee
Life As A Kid

14: Mar~Apr '96
£4.00
Bruce Reynolds
Will Self

15: May~Jun '96
SOLD OUT
Hashish Killers
Alex Chilton

16: Aug~Sept '96
SOLD OUT
John Michel
World Poker

17: Nov~Dec '96
SOLD OUT
John Cooper Clarke
Cary Grant

18: Spring '97
SOLD OUT
Thomas Pynchon
Ivan Illich

19: Summer '97
£4.00
Psychogeography
Henry Miller

20: Winter '97
SOLD OUT
Howard Marks
Kenny Kramer

21: Feb~March '98
SOLD OUT
The Gambler
Bez

22: April~May '98
SOLD OUT
Alan Moore
Alex James

23: June~July '98
SOLD OUT
Summer Special
Tim Roth

24: Aug~Sep '98
SOLD OUT
Krazy Golf
David Soul

MAN'S RUIN 25: Winter 1999
£15
The first book-format Idler, featuring Louis Theroux's Sick Notes, Will Self, Howard Marks, Adam and Joe and Ken Kesey

PARADISE 26: Summer 2000
£5
Jonathan Coe meets David Nobbs, Nicholas Blincoe on Sherlock Holmes, Tiki Special, Iain Sinclair on the London Eye

THE FOOL 27: Winter 2000
£5
Village Idiots, World Of Pain, Arthur Smith's diary, The Big Quit, James Jarvis's World of Pain, John Lloyd

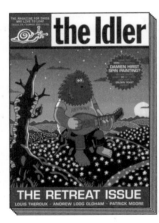

RETREAT 28: Summer 2001
£10
Louis Theroux meets Bill Oddie, Jonathan Ross meets Alan Moore, Alex James meets Patrick Moore, plus Andrew Loog Oldham

HELL 29: Winter 2001
£10
Crass founder Penny Rimbaud, Crap Jobs Special, Boredom Section, New fiction from Niall Griffiths, Mark Manning, Billy Childish

LOVE 30: Summer 2002
£10
Louis Theroux meets Colin Wilson, Johnny Ball on Descartes, Crap Towns, Devon Retreat, Chris Yates interview, Marchesa Casati